Management Consulting Projects

This textbook provides students with an easy to use, proven roadmap for completing a successful consulting project from start to finish.

Primarily designed for students who work as outside consultants on solving client problems and investigating potential opportunities, the textbook's structure first explains the consulting process to students and then depicts it in a chronological flow, using real-life examples to demonstrate practical application. Each section builds upon the previous one, focusing on the development of critical thinking, problem solving, and communication skills for employability. Now in its sixth edition, this text has been fully revised to bring it up to date with the current business context and global environment, including:

- A major expansion of the tools and resources needed for students to conduct research on a client's situation.
- A new final chapter that ties the overarching consulting process together and focuses on how the student should use this experience for their own professional development.
- New examples of award-winning projects to provide practical guidance.
- Fresh material on the use of new technologies in the consulting process, ethics and data management, and remote working.

This well-renowned model promotes a conceptual understanding of the consulting process and the interactions between and among students, the team, the client, and the instructor. *Management Consulting Projects* should be essential reading for experiential Business Consulting modules, Small Business Management, and Strategic Management at postgraduate and MBA level.

Ronald Cook is the Associate Dean for Graduate Business and an Entrepreneurship Professor at the Norm Brodsky College of Business, Rider University, USA.

Michael Harris is the J. Fielding Miller Distinguished Professor and Director of the Miller School of Entrepreneurship in the College of Business at East Carolina University, USA.

Dennis Barber III is an Assistant Professor of Management in the College of Business at East Carolina University, USA.

Management Consulting Projects

A Step-by-Step Experiential Guide

Sixth edition

Ronald Cook, Michael Harris
and Dennis Barber III

LONDON AND NEW YORK

Sixth edition published 2022
by Routledge
2 Park Square, Milton Park, Abingdon, Oxon, OX14 4RN

and by Routledge
605 Third Avenue, New York, NY 10158

Routledge is an imprint of the Taylor & Francis Group, an informa business

First edition published by Thomson 2006
Fifth edition published by Cengage 2016

British Library Cataloguing-in-Publication Data
A catalogue record for this book is available from the British Library

Library of Congress Cataloging-in-Publication Data
Names: Cook, Ronald G., author. | Harris, Michael, 1970– author.
Title: Management consulting projects: a step-by-step experiential guide / Ronald Cook, Michael Harris and Dennis Barber III.
Other titles: Experiential student team consulting process.
Description: Sixth Edition. | New York: Routledge, 2021. | Revised edition of The experiential student team consulting process, c2016. | Includes bibliographical references and index.
Identifiers: LCCN 2021007747 (print) | LCCN 2021007748 (ebook)
Subjects: LCSH: Business consultants—Training of—Handbooks, manuals, etc. | Experiential learning—Study and teaching—Handbooks, manuals, etc.
Classification: LCC HD69.C6 C663 2021 (print) | LCC HD69.C6 (ebook) | DDC 001—dc23
LC record available at https://lccn.loc.gov/2021007747
LC ebook record available at https://lccn.loc.gov/2021007748

ISBN: 978-1-032-00515-7 (hbk)
ISBN: 978-1-032-00516-4 (pbk)
ISBN: 978-1-003-17451-6 (ebk)

Typeset in Optima
by codeMantra

Contents

About the authors

Dr. Ronald Cook is the Associate Dean for Graduate Business and Entrepreneurship Professor at the Norm Brodsky College of Business, Rider University. He was the founding director of Rider's Center for Entrepreneurial Studies and founded and runs Rider's Small Business Institute®, where his student consulting teams have earned multiple national and regional awards for excellence. As Associate Dean, he manages the five graduate business degree programs and is part of the leadership team for the AACSB-accredited college. In his discipline, he develops and teaches undergraduate and graduate courses in team-based small business consulting, entrepreneurship/small business, new venture planning, and corporate entrepreneurship. Ron is a member, a Fellow, a Mentor, and past president of the Small Business Institute® association. He has published a number of award-winning articles on small business and entrepreneurship and was the recipient of Rider University's Distinguished Teaching Award. He is the lead author on the previous five editions. https://www.rider.edu/faculty/ronald-cook

Dr. Michael L. Harris is the J. Fielding Miller Distinguished Professor and Director of the Miller School of Entrepreneurship in the College of Business at East Carolina University (ECU). He is a Fellow and Past President of the National Small Business Institute®, and Co-Editor-in-Chief of the *Journal of Small Business Strategy*. In his small business consulting course, Dr. Harris has worked with over 700 students to complete 135 consulting projects for local small business clients since 2000. His teams have won numerous awards in the National Small Business Institute® Project-of-the-Year competition, including multiple first place finishes. In addition, he received a $1 million grant from the Golden LEAF Foundation in 2019 to support rural economic prosperity through innovation and entrepreneurship. Dr. Harris has won several teaching awards at ECU, including the College of Business Teacher-Scholar Award, Alumni Teaching Award, and the Board of Governor's Distinguished Professor Award. He is a new co-author. https://business.ecu.edu/faculty/harrismi/

Dr. Dennis Barber III is an Assistant Professor in the Miller School of Entrepreneurship in the College of Business at East Carolina University. He currently serves on the board of directors for the national Small Business Institute® and is a Managing Editor of the *Journal of Small Business Strategy*. Since 2014, Dr. Barber has been leading student consulting teams in small business and family business courses accumulating over 15,000 hours of student service-learning hours. His students have won multiple National Small Business Institute® Project-of-the-Year competition awards, and Dr. Barber has been recognized as a thought leader for his best practices with student consulting teams. He is a former Entrepreneurship Teaching and Learning Scholar with the United States Association for Small Business and Entrepreneurship where he currently serves as the Chair for the Rural Entrepreneurship Special Interest Group. He has published over 20 peer-reviewed papers on topics such as entrepreneurship education, rural entrepreneurship, entrepreneurial attitudes, public policy, and small business strategy. He is a new co-author. https://business.ecu.edu/faculty/barberde/

Preface

Welcome to the sixth edition of *Managing Consulting Projects: A Step-by-Step Experiential Guide*.

Ron Cook, Mike Harris, and Dennis Barber III are experts in the field of Managerial Consulting, delivered using student teams in an experiential learning approach. Experiential student consulting often takes place in capstone courses and requires instructors to take a clinical, rather than classroom, approach. We share a passion for the experiential consulting process and the desire to contribute to the improvement of the student, client, and instructor experiences. By sharing our best practices in these pages, we provide you with in-depth, how-to knowledge, and examples, tools, and templates that you can readily use in your own consulting process experience. This book should be most helpful in meeting the integrative demands of your experiential learning. Additional resources are available in our Instructor's manual.

We describe our experiential process in Chapter 1. Chapters 2 through 5 are devoted to the four phases in our Process Flow Model: Consulting Team Development, Client Issues, Contract and Relationship Management, and Project Deliverables. Chapter 6 concludes with Professional Development suggestions for students, whereas the Appendices contain more than a dozen templates and examples for your use.

***New in this edition**: This edition welcomes two new co-authors who bring an additional 20+ years of teaching student consulting using an experimental process approach. Along with two new award-winning project examples in our appendix, we offer four major additions to further help students and instructors cope with the intricacies of this kind of learning:*

- *The first is to redesign the Process Flow Model to clarify what the steps an instructor will take and those areas where the students are the responsible parties, as well as refine the chronological nature of the consulting engagement.*
- *The second is to expand the understanding of the client's issues through root cause analysis so the letter of engagement can be more effective.*
- *The third is a new chapter on professional development for the student. One of the key benefits of experiential consulting is the growth of the students. By being consultants to a client, students apply the skills in a real-world setting and can use this experience to differentiate themselves in the workplace.*
- *An Instructor's manual is now available with guidance on the role of mentors, and pre and post classroom activities.*

We also need to acknowledge and thank three individuals for their contributions. The first is the executive vice president of Spruce Industries, Dan Josephs. Spruce was the client for the consulting project in Appendix 2F. The second is the Jordan Bogue of Elite Boutique, the client for the project in Appendix 2G. The third is the co-author of the previous edition, Diane Campbell. While not involved in this edition, her contributions to the text will not be forgotten. Finally, we would like to thank the team of external reviewers for their feedback as we developed the sixth edition.

This book is written to help students by providing conceptual and practical process models that they can adopt for use in their own projects. Clients should find it helpful to understand the experiential student team consulting process when participating in a consulting program. We share our best practices with instructors to offer a pedagogically sound, integrative approach to experiential learning. Enjoy!

Introduction

This textbook can be used by students and instructors while working with clients in consulting projects. It is based on an accumulation of best practices in student team consulting gained from directing hundreds of students who have worked on numerous projects. Teams using our models have won many awards for their consulting reports.

Students are the primary audience for this text. The textbook first explains the consulting process and then depicts it in a chronological flow. Students should read the entire text as they begin a consulting engagement. Once teams are formed and the consulting process is underway, they should revisit each section as needed. Furthermore, students are encouraged to examine the appendices closely. The appendices provide invaluable resources through the templates and examples.

Instructors can use this book to help the project flow and reference appropriate chapter(s) as the consulting process unfolds. In addition, instructors can utilize the examples in the appendix and the instructor's manual to organize the course.

Instructors could also provide a copy of the text to each client involved in their program and request that the client read it prior to the consulting engagement, as a successful project requires clear communication of the consulting process among all parties. When a client signs up for a student consulting program, they may not understand the difference between a student consulting team and a professional consultant, or they might consider the experiential student team consulting process like an internship. Clients should understand this process, their responsibilities as clients, and how they can help enhance the students' learning experience.

Experiential student team consulting, referred to in this text as STC, is one of the best learning tools for students. We believe that the practical knowledge and experience gained by participating in these programs is unmatched in higher education. Because it involves three parties operating in a real-world environment, there is learning that occurs that cannot be found in a classroom-based course. This textbook is designed to help facilitate that learning.

Experiential learning using consulting

Abstract

In this chapter, you will find a definition of experiential student team consulting, a discussion of the importance of experiential learning, an explanation of the different types of consulting, a conceptual framework, the purpose of fieldwork, and considerations of confidentiality and ethics.

Definition

Student team consulting has become an invaluable experiential learning program for undergraduate and graduate business students at or near the completion of their academic careers. In 1971, Rutgers University established one of the first programs of its kind in the United States, the Rutgers MBA Team Consulting Program (Rutgers, 2003). In 1972, the Small Business Institute® (SBI) program began as a cooperative venture between colleges and universities and the U.S. Small Business Administration. At its peak, fieldwork, as it was commonly called, grew to encompass over 400 schools (Matthews, 1998). A number of other institutions continue to provide similar offerings of experiential student team consulting as a multi-discipline, capstone course or as an integral part of another course. These field experiences, some required, others elective, allowed students to integrate their academic and life skills in a problem-solving or consulting endeavor with real clients who will benefit from the solutions developed.

Fieldwork is faculty-guided, experiential student consulting. What is meant by that? In part, this process can be explained by telling what it is not. It is not an internship where a student works under someone's direct supervision for "x" hours a week, academic credit, and, perhaps, pay. It is not a hypothetical project or case that may be in a textbook. Fieldwork involves an actual client and a real situation. It can best be described by picturing a company hiring an outside consultant. The consultant needs to understand the issues facing the client, devise a contract with the client, and then execute the contract. When a consultant begins to work with a client, all the needed information may not be available, and what is available can be inaccurate. Students must also deal with this kind of ambiguity, just as the consultant does. Student team consulting places you in real-world situations where they address the real-world needs of their clients (Greiner & Metzger, 1983).

Consulting is all about problem-solving. In the initial stages of a consulting engagement, underlying causes of the client's problem are often unknown. The consultant must search the evidence, read the clues, and define the problems.

Types of consultants

There are several basic types of consultants, and we will focus on two: process and content, and the approaches (diagnostic and implementation) that can be used with these two. As noted by Porth and Saltis (1998),

> Process consultants encourage their clients to identify their own problems and formulate their own solutions through a series of questions and guidance.... A content consultant is more like a surgeon, in that they take a direct approach to diagnose the problem and develop a corrective action.... The consultant performs all phases of the process, and presents a preferred solution to the client.... A diagnostic approach identifies the causes of problems and recommends a course of action to solve the problem. However, this process stops short at this point and does not see the recommended changes through to fruition. The implementation approach includes the actual execution of the proposed changes.
>
> (p. 29)

Student team consulting is typically done using a content approach rather than a process approach, as students do not act as a counselor to the client as is done in the process approach. A student team usually researches the problem and presents a solution to the client. The solution presented is then considered diagnostic because it would stop short of implementation. As students operate under an academic calendar, and must wrap up projects fairly quickly, they typically do not see the "rest of the story" and do not implement their recommendations to the client. In contrast, small business consultants in non-academic settings may implement their recommended changes as part of their contract with the client.

Experiential learning

Experiential learning is a broad category that encompasses a range of learning activities from internships to consulting projects to student-run ventures. It is considered more holistic than classroom-only instruction and helps bridge the gap between what the students learn passively and the actual job expectations that students encounter when they enter the working world (Maskulka, Stout, & Massad, 2011).

This text is about experiential learning using student team consulting to gain knowledge, and then demonstrating how the consulting process enhances student learning. As stated by Kickul, Griffiths, and Bacq (2010), to gain genuine knowledge from an experience, certain abilities are required:

- the learner must be willing to be actively involved in the experience;
- the learner must possess and use analytical skills to conceptualize the experience;
- the learner must possess decision-making and problem-solving skills to use the new ideas gained from the experience; and,
- the learner must be able to reflect on the experience (p. 654).

Specifically, the methodology used in experiential student team consulting is called problem-based learning (PBL; Brownell & Jameson, 2004). What better way to prepare you for the "real world" than to engage in a consulting process? As noted by Peterson (2004), when discussing PBL:

> in the workplace, problems are ill structured, ambiguous, messy, complex, and most often do not have one correct answer that can be found at the end of the book in the answer key…. These types of

> problems provide a powerful learning opportunity.... This new learning paradigm also makes the learning process messy.... No longer is the path to success clear. This paradigm requires that the students first identify what the real problem is, next identify what they know and need to know, and then identify viable solutions through both creative and critical thinking.
>
> (p. 632)

Furthermore, in consulting projects, students often discover that the client's business decisions are not always made on a rational basis and, instead, find an emotional justification. As a result, PBL projects also offer the possibility of "eureka" moments, where students learn about less-than-ideal business decision-making (Brownell & Jameson, 2004). Part of the reason consulting has a certain level of ambiguity is that the client may rely on "gut instincts" to make decisions (another way to characterize emotional justifications), and there can be information gaps due to incomplete or inaccurate reporting. The client will likely be reporting in good faith, but part of the problem can be these errors. This is a common problem in management, and consulting gives a good introduction to this issue. A crucial part of the consulting process is learning how to manage ambiguity.

In conducting fieldwork, students will operate under this type of uncertainty. Since fieldwork involves a client and a real-life experience, the situation will likely be fluid and information may change over the course of the consulting assignment. Therefore, as noted in the above explanation of PBL, fieldwork requires an integrated, holistic approach that examines the issues from different business perspectives, as well as from different functional disciplines. Students will learn that there can be multiple solutions and discern when to change your mindset from one of inquiry, i.e., questioning the pros and cons of multiple approaches, to one of advocacy, i.e., picking one approach from the range of alternatives and then making a strong case for that choice. PBL methodology allows you to research unstructured, complex problems. These types of problems require you to define the issues, develop alternative solutions, and pick an option (Brownell & Jameson, 2004).

The student team consulting model shares some similarities with service-learning pedagogy, as both

> seek to balance academic rigor with a practical relevance which furnishes students with a broader and, we argue, richer, educational

> experience. They address one of the most salient criticisms of business education today – the absence of realistic experience, applied learning, and grounded personal development.
>
> (Godfrey, Illes, & Berry, 2005, p. 311)

Fieldwork is thus an excellent mechanism to improve research abilities and critical thinking skills. As Brownell and Jamison (2004) state:

> Fieldwork provides an interdisciplinary catalyst to motivate students' cognitive and affective learning but also as an impetus for skills-oriented learning by providing team tasks that interweave challenges from several disciplines. A well-chosen problem yields a group of team tasks that requires integrated learning rather than fragmented learning. An interdisciplinary approach is realistic because business problems usually cut across typical curricular boundaries. Thus, PBL encourages students to develop implementation skills that mirror those required to meet future challenges that they will face.
>
> (p. 561)

Hence, students will be challenged to not only discover information about a particular issue but, in many cases, determine if this issue is important at all. From an anonymous course evaluation, one student consultant noted:

> Unlike a regular course where we are told to read chapter 6 and answer questions 1–5, the consulting experience required us to consider whether chapter 6 even mattered and if so, which questions were important. More than anything else, we learned to ask good questions.

Because of this inherent need to ask good questions, students' research included synthesizing materials from a wide variety of sources. Through the learning techniques utilized in the consulting process, students learned how to imply important business concepts, how companies functioned, and how methods of inquiry help clarify complex business situations (Brownell & Jameson, 2004).

The educational process is much more than memorizing a set of facts and figures. It is about lifelong learning and equipping the student with the skills to handle ambiguous situations. Fieldwork does just that.

Fieldwork projects can vary based on the time and complexity of the consulting assignment and whether these projects are part of other classes or are a separate course. Regardless of their structure, all projects typically involve a client, instructor, and students. The interplay of these groups constitutes the framework for learning.

Conceptual framework

The experiential student team consulting model has four constituencies: the client, the student team, the student, and the instructor, as depicted in Figure 1.1. This model represents all the players in an experiential student team consulting environment.

The client (C) represents the firm/organization who will be the beneficiary of the consulting engagement. Depending on the size of the firm, the client can be more than one person (or single point of contact), but, under most consulting assignments, there is usually one client-point person. The client typically works initially with the instructor setting up the project parameters, then with the team during the semester, and finally with the team and the instructor to wrap up the engagement, often at the final presentation.

The circle S represents the student consultant as an individual involved in the consulting process. The student works within the team (T). The team interacts with the client, the instructor, and among its individual members. In viewing the model, the individual student (S) and the client never interact because this is a student team consulting process. Under this consulting framework, the team is considered the consulting professional, and the viewpoints expressed to the client by the team's contact person (the team

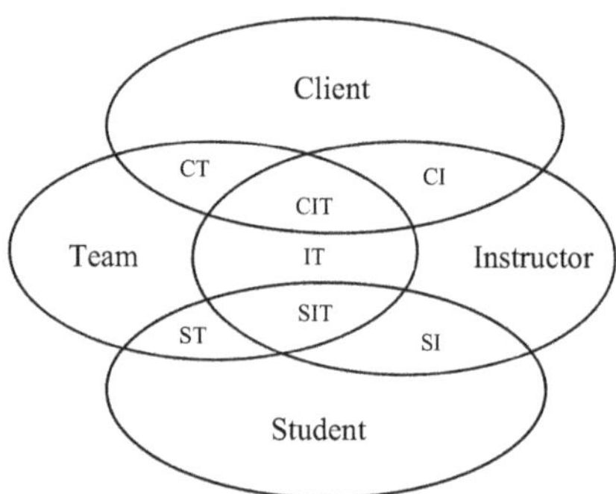

Figure 1.1 Experiential student team consulting model.

leader) represents the team's position and are not necessarily the opinion of any individual student.

The instructor (I) has the opening role in the process as they coordinate with the client initially and often set up the student team. There is usually an initial meeting for the class where all students meet to discuss the syllabus and course rules. If the consulting project is part of a class (not a separate course), the rest of the class will meet in its normal fashion during the semester. For separate consulting courses, the instructor facilitates the team during the consulting engagement, interacts with each student individually, and concludes the consulting course. Student interactions with the instructor begin when the consulting assignments are being structured, during any points in the engagement where individual grading occurs, and if problems arise. The time constraints of the academic calendar will help determine how proactive the instructor needs to be regarding problem-solving regarding client or team issues.

The next focus is on the model's multiple interactions, which provide an understanding of how the consulting process works. There are seven interactions, represented by overlapping circles in the model. The team and the instructor have a greater role, as measured by the number of possible interactions, at five each. The client and the student each have three interaction possibilities. It is important to note that while the interactions discussed below are described as occurring face-to-face, recent events (the pandemic) required most schools to switch to a period of remote learning. The authors experienced that pivot as well, and used remote synchronous in place of face-to-face meetings. Hence, the processes described below can be achieved using remote synchronous tools like Zoom, Google Meet, and so on.

The area CT represents the client and team interactions. These interactions occur during the regular course of a consulting engagement and are both formal and informal. Formal interactions would be activities like site visits to the client, client progress reports, and the final presentation. An informal interaction could be an information request to the client. The area CI represents the client and instructor interaction to set up the consulting engagement, prior to the project beginning, and then at the end of the assignment when the client is asked to evaluate the quality of the team's work. During the consulting engagement, the client and the instructor would not usually interact. The instructor is more of a behind-the-scenes facilitator or coach for the team. The area CIT is where the client, instructor, and team all interact. Some engagements may have interim reports to the client, and, generally, all consulting engagements will have a formal presentation to the client done at the end of the project. In addition, CIT interactions can also occur informally as a troubleshooting mechanism, when there is a problem with the team and the client which requires the instructor to bring all parties together.

The highest frequency of interactions usually occurs in the area IT, the core of experiential learning. This is because of the nature of the student team consulting model. Your team will be in regular communication with the instructor, both reporting on the progress of the consulting engagement and receiving guidance on how to be consultants. The frequency will vary depending on the engagement and the instructor's preferences. A typical frequency for face-to-face interactions is at least weekly, with email or phone conversations occurring more often.

In contrast, IS area interactions generally occur twice: first, in the beginning when the team is created and second, in the end to determine student grades. Other IS interactions are likely to occur only if the student has a problem with the team, another student on the team, or if there are some circumstances where special assistance to the student is needed. The SIT area is for interactions that occur when there is a major disagreement between the team and one or more of its members. These interactions are rare but, if needed, it typically is because there are such serious disagreements in the team (perhaps a student has either quit or been removed) and the instructor needs to call all parties together to work out a solution. The last interaction area of our model is ST. Here, issues of team dynamics come into play. Students will be developing a team structure that will include a team leader, team norms, and so on, and this area is a forum for these discussions. It is important to remember that PBL emphasizes that each student must be responsible for their own learning. This happens in student team consulting through the team structure. Students work in teams so that collective insight will offset individual limitations (Brownell & Jameson, 2004).

What is not represented in the model is the role of an outside mentor to the team. This is because the use of a mentor is an optional activity and may not occur in all consulting situations. Mentoring is a process where information is communicated informally, usually face-to-face and for a sustained period of time, between a person who is perceived to have greater relevant knowledge, wisdom, or experience (the mentor) and a person who is perceived to have less of these (the mentee). For mentorship to be effective, it is important that the mentee believe that the mentor has the best interests of the mentee at heart (Bozeman & Sweeney, 2007).

As most students involved in the student consulting process have likely not been consultants before, the students are learning this process and, at the same time, acting as consultants. Depending on the nature of the class, the students typically meet with the instructor to discuss/review the work on their project, gain feedback from the instructor, ask questions, and so on, often in a seminar-type format. Having a mentor involved in these discussions and available to the students provides a number of advantages.

First, regardless of the knowledge base of the team or the instructor, the mentor can bring a whole new set of knowledge, skills, and abilities to the consulting project. They can connect the students to new resources, contacts, and so on that can help the student team do a better job on their project. Second, the mentor will develop a relationship with the team and can be used as a sounding board for new ideas, reviewing assignments before submission, and generally answering questions that a student might feel awkward asking their instructor. Third, consulting projects typically have a formal presentation to the client. The student team can have the mentor provide feedback to them in rehearsals, rather than have the instructor do this, as the instructor will ultimately be grading the student and students may feel uncomfortable rehearsing with the instructor. This feeling can occur even if the instructor assures the student that they are not being graded on the rehearsals and the practice presentation is just that: practice. Finally, the mentor can help improve team dynamics during the consulting engagement as they are a neutral third party who is familiar with the team and the project and can help resolve potential conflicts.

Purpose of fieldwork

Student team consulting offers you an opportunity to integrate your academic and work experiences in the creation of a consulting solution for a client's real-world problem. The consulting course provides you with experiential learning in small group dynamics, problem definition, research methodology and application, project management, and in making presentations. In many respects, the course is like a sandbox, where you get to be creative and inventive but in a disciplined manner.

Since the purpose of any consulting engagement should be to improve the client's condition, clients are encouraged to actively participate in the student consulting process (see the model) and thereby gain useful recommendations. However, unlike professional consultants, students are usually less experienced in consulting and will be learning about the consulting process as they work on the assignment.

Another important difference between student and non-student consulting is the need for students and clients to follow the calendar of the academic institution. Typically, this is not onerous. Rather, it means that there are identifiable beginning and ending points (along with holidays and other breaks) that are defined by the academic calendar. The main concerns are the scope of the project that can be accepted (it must be able to be done in a limited time frame) and the ability to adapt for contingencies if something goes wrong, as more resources cannot usually be added to the project if problems occur. Good planning at the start can allow for this.

Ethical considerations

In addition to adhering to the code of ethics of their academic institution, students, clients, and instructors need to conduct themselves in such a way that business ethics are strictly observed. If the consulting engagement's methodology calls for primary research, you must clearly identify yourself as a student in a consulting course conducting research for the benefit of your client. Students should also attest that they have no conflicts of interest with the client's business. Such conflicts can include family members (including self) owning a business that competes with the client or recommending services to the client in which you have a financial interest. In addition, students should affirm that they have no rights to any improvements to the client's condition that may result from the consulting engagement. It is central to the integrity of the student team consulting process that this kind of full disclosure never be compromised.

An additional important component with regards to ethics is the vetting and validating of information and data used in the report. Though Google is a powerful tool, it does not present data from only valid sources. You should make an extra effort to ensure that the recommendations suggested are supported by credible data sources. More of this will be discussed in the third chapter. Once the credibility of sources has been established and recommendations are formed, it is important to ensure that all assertions made in the report have a logical or empirical foundation. Remember that the client may implement the recommendations, and students are ethically responsible for providing credible, grounded, and actionable recommendations.

Confidentiality

Another hallmark of student team consulting is the maintenance of confidentiality. Its purpose is to commit the students and instructor to treating all materials received and developed during the consulting engagement as the confidential property of the client. While on-site (if that is the case), all pictures of the client's operations must be approved by the client for use in any place other than the consulting report.

Occasionally, a client may have a situation involving intellectual property that counsel advises be covered by a non-standard agreement drawn up by the attorney and client. In such instances, the instructor will obtain the institution's advice on using the non-standard form, and students should be free to consult their own attorneys. While the client's rights may justify special treatment, neither the institution nor the students can be unfairly restricted in their future endeavors. Most institutions use a standard form that discusses ethical considerations and confidentiality, like the example in Appendix 1B.

Students may receive confidential information via email. Before this information is shared with other team members, it must be password-protected and only be sent through an encrypted email. Please contact the information technology department at your university for more guidance. You will want to ensure that the client knows of these practices and that you will employ them as you initially share confidential information.

Communication

Another attribute of a good consultant is effective communication. An accurate exchange of information, opinions, and feelings between the client and the consultant is a critical skill for all consultants (Cherrington, 1995) because "In the small business setting, the consultant must not only possess these communication skills, but also be a 'straight shooter.' Small business consultants must have the freedom and courage to challenge the assumptions and perceptions of the owner/manager" (Porth & Saltis, 1998, p. 45). In a non-academic setting, consultants may fear losing business if they tell the client something that the client does not want to hear. However, being a "straight-shooter" will help build the trust needed for any effective consulting relationship, and for students, it is easier to speak the truth as you are not concerned about losing a client, as your focus is on learning. You may feel reluctant to relay 'bad news', but communicating honestly when the situation is uncomfortable is also a very valuable learning experience.

As students begin their consulting assignment, there should be a chronological flow to its approach. We developed this process flow model to help students understand the experiential student team consulting (STC) process. Figure 1.2 illustrates the complete model, and each main student segment will be detailed in a separate chapter.

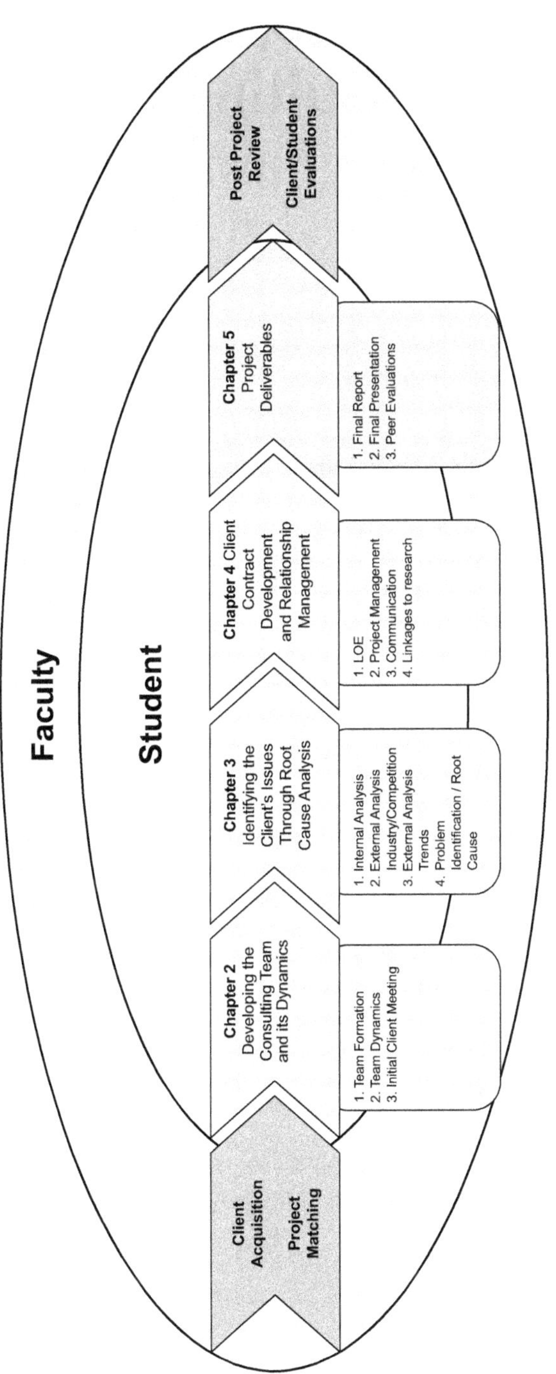

Figure 1.2 Process flow.

Developing the consulting team and its dynamics

Abstract

The team approach is critical to student consulting. Although each team member has ideas about how to approach a client's problem, the team context requires you to learn from each other as well as to negotiate to reach a solution. Communication between team members, your professor, and client are all vital for a high-quality experience and top-notch deliverables.

Your instructor has front-end and back-end work to set up the experience and to assess the results. Finding appropriate client projects and matching them with student teams help ensure that the teams are well balanced and the skills match the client's needs. This chapter focuses on the first aspect of the process where students are involved. Developing the team dynamics and setting expectations early lead to less confusion among the group. "By collaborating, each team capitalizes on its members' individual strengths and expertise. Teams also learn to handle inevitable disagreements and conflicts" (Brownell & Jameson, 2004, p. 560).

Project matching

Project matching can occur simultaneously with team formation. However, the process here is explained sequentially. Hence, students may face one of three situations:

1. The instructor has assigned a client company to you.
2. Client companies have been selected by the instructor for the project teams, but students may request a different team/client if they have a specific reason for doing so.
3. Students choose from a portfolio of client projects, and teams are formed based on who wants to work with a specific client.

In many circumstances, the instructor simply assigns students to both teams and clients, and we depict it in Figure 1.2 in Chapter 1 in that fashion. If it is the third option, clients will come to the school and make a presentation to the student consultants about their organization and their needs. In these cases, the client is not guaranteed a student team if their project is not picked. In all options, you can expect the instructors to check for team balance and skills, adjusting as necessary with or without negotiation with the students. Sometimes there is an additional element where a group of students have a pre-existing study group and wish to keep that group intact for the consulting course. When possible, these wishes can be respected, if the skills balance and a match with clients can be achieved.

Team formation

The team formation activity often happens simultaneously with project matching, and student consulting teams typically have from two to five members. The team size depends in part on the magnitude of the consulting project, the size of the class, and the length of the academic term (most consulting projects are one semester in length). While team size can be larger than five, doing so typically requires a team leader/coordinator who manages the workflow of the other students. As a result, larger teams do require different dynamics. To aid in the creation of teams, instructors may use a background or profile questionnaire that is completed by students after registration but before the first class. Instructors then use this information to balance team skills, academic disciplines, career interests, and experience while evaluating the client project assignments. Although it is somewhat of an inexact science, team formation needs to balance a mix of student skills, a client fit, and, to the extent possible, student choice.

Team dynamics/communication

Clarity between your team and the client is key for an effective consulting relationship, particularly when serving a smaller organization. As noted by Porth and Saltis (1998),

> First, much more so than for a large organization, the future of a small business frequently rests squarely on the ability of one, or at most a few individuals, to be clear about strategy, tactics, and resources. Second, a small business does not generally have the same capacity to check, test, and analyze recommendations that a large business does. Large organizations tend to be inherently more bureaucratic. The benefit of a bureaucracy is that it maintains the status quo, and provides a series of check and balances, a gauntlet, that any change must pass through before being implemented. This series of checks and balances rarely exist in a small business. A small business must be more focused and clearer about the outcomes (i.e., value), methods, and resources required for any project or activity. Third, a small business must act much more quickly than a large organization since a small business does not have the same resource cushion. If time is money in a large business, it is much more so to a small business. A small business simply cannot afford to take a great deal of time in making changes.
>
> (pp. 36–37)

Team dynamics consists of several issues, ranging from organization to communication to conflict. To begin, once formed, teams need to organize themselves. Specifically, you need to select a team leader and possibly a treasurer and administrator. The team leader will serve as the point person for communications with your client, and the team will determine how communication (formal and informal) will be handled. Let us reemphasize this point: Each team should have one member (leader) who is the main contact person with the client. Your client should know who to contact if a question arises. You should also have a secondary contact person. A typical contact form that can be filled out and left with your client is shown in Appendix 1C.

If the team is large (five or more students), there is also an enhanced need for coordination. The team leader can also assume the role of team coordinator, assuring the flow of the team's work, and will most likely take on less of the project workload. If you have a team administrator, that person will be responsible for taking and disseminating minutes of all team meetings and collecting and summarizing weekly activity reports. It is possible that one person can serve as leader and administrator, but experience suggests that the team leader not have other, simultaneous team roles (other than coordinator). You may have a need for a treasurer if there are any monetary issues. Monetary issues may include reimbursement for travel, funding for duplication or survey expenses, and so on. Depending on the situation, reimbursement would come from the client or the school. Therefore, the treasurer would collect receipts and process the team's expense reimbursement from the appropriate party. It is reasonable to combine the administrator and treasurer functions or not have a treasurer if there are no monetary issues. There may be other formal group roles, depending on team size.

An additional task once teams are formed is to decide the medium, nature, and frequency of communications among its members. In addition to the standard email and phone use, learning management systems such as Blackboard® and Canvas® serve a useful role in facilitating a learning environment. They are typically available for each class at a school and offer common information exchange areas, secure group sections, and the ability to host interactive chat rooms. Furthermore, other third-party tools (Google Drive, etc.) can also serve as a resource. Basically, students are encouraged to adopt whatever methods that will allow them to achieve effective communications.

Perhaps the most common concern with teams is conflict. Conflict can be an inevitable part of your experience, but it doesn't have to be just a source of tension and distraction (Warters, 2000). It can lead to a way of resolving differences and responding to issues that are causing friction. Conflict can direct the group in ways that members would not have anticipated earlier. Conflict can also be something that tears a group apart and that increases tension among members. However, "if people express their feelings and needs in a positive and constructive way, it reduces anxiety and prevents escalation of conflict" (Gill, Heermans, & Herath, 1998, p. 6).

When your team is trying to resolve conflict, it is important to strive toward a win-win solution, as conflict resolution need not result in 'winners and losers'. There are two basic methods to deal with conflict that can get you to a win-win result: compromise and mediation.

Compromise emphasizes both sides giving up something they want to reach a middle ground. This is a good method to use when both parties are willing to listen to the other's position and is handled by the team itself.

Mediation uses a neutral third party to assist the team members in voluntarily reaching of an agreement. Mediation assumes that the parties know their positions the best and enables them to come up with their own solution. Mediation focuses on things team members can change. For example, you do not try to change someone's beliefs or values. Rather, you change tasks or plans (Gill, Heermans, & Herath, 1998).

There are numerous types of problems that may cause conflict among your team. A brief discussion of some of the more common problems and suggestions for what to do about them follows:

1. Frustration over size of project – at the start of a project, a team can be overwhelmed by the amount of work necessary to complete it. At this point, you are often thinking of the project as an individual endeavor rather than as a group one. The team may not realize that the work will be divided up and is much easier to handle than they first believed. One of the first things to do to overcome this frustration is to divide the project into sub-tasks. Use a project management chart (see the discussion in Chapter 4) and brainstorm all the sub-tasks that will need to be completed in order to finish the project. Establish individual responsibility and deadlines for each sub-task (Lyons, 2003).
2. Unbalanced participation from team members – if one or two individuals dominate the group discussion, the team will lose its most valuable commodity – the variety of opinions and ideas expressed by its members. While some people are naturally more talkative or comfortable in group situations than others, everyone on the team should be encouraged to participate and no one should be allowed to control all of the discussion. To offset this, try teambuilding activities in which success requires participation from all members in order to draw out the more reserved members. This may open lines of communication and put members more at ease when talking to and sharing ideas with each other. Furthermore, the group could have someone assume the role of gatekeeper during each meeting. The gatekeeper's job is to make sure everyone is given a chance to speak and that no one person dominates the conversation (Lyons, 2003).
3. Frustration over lack of progress – when a project takes a long time to complete, you may feel as though the end will never come and you have not accomplished anything. This frustration can also occur when you come across a problem you are having trouble solving. One way to overcome this is to check off the tasks that have been completed from

the project management chart, and then you can see how much they have accomplished. You can also ask each member to list two things they have done for the project so far and two things they still need to do. Someone in the team can record the team's accomplishments and all the remaining work. If you are really frustrated, then step away from the project for a few minutes. Do something else for 15 minutes to get your mind off of the project (Gill, Heermans, & Herath, 1998).

4. Resistance to being a team – there are many reasons why you may resist being part of a team. You may have had negative team experiences in the past, might fear rejection of your ideas, or may not trust other team members. People who are resistant to working in a team often agree to any idea to get the project done quicker. Furthermore, when people resist being part of the team, they might work on the project on their own and, therefore, not be sharing their ideas. As a result, other team members might think that some students are freeriding and become resentful. At a minimum, the group loses a valuable resource.

   In general, teambuilding activities that allow members to get to know each other are good for increasing comfort levels within the team. By setting deadlines and asking everyone to give an update of their section of the project at each meeting, team members can keep track of each other. This ensures that everyone is doing their part of the work and helps those members who are afraid they will have to do more than their fair share of the work. If many of the people on your team have had negative group experiences in the past, have everyone list two positive things about working with a team. Discuss how you can incorporate those characteristics into your team. You can also have each member name one thing that went wrong with a previous team and discuss how you can avoid having the same problem arise within your team. Establish norms that ensure each member has the opportunity to speak openly and candidly (Gill, Heermans, & Herath, 1998).

5. Separating fact from opinion – when people feel strongly about something, they often will state their personal opinions as facts. While opinions can be very useful in a team, they must be regarded as subjective, and you must recognize that not everyone will agree with an opinion. It is important that your team is objective and critical when dealing with opinions so that you do not proceed on unreliable information. A group norm can be instituted where everyone must back their opinions with facts or sources. To implement this, your group could have someone

assume the role of devil's advocate at each meeting. This person should question all statements and give opposing viewpoints so that other team members are required to make sound arguments and think through their statements (Lyons, 2003).

In summary, you and your team may have different expectations of the project itself, the level of commitment expected of others, and the level of effort they plan on expending. Dealing with these issues upfront is important for the team. Generally, conflict in student teams is not a question of if it will occur, it is more a question of when it will occur. Setting the expectations of the project upfront may set the tone for handling further problems. If you find that you cannot resolve differences in the beginning when everyone is polite and cordial, when the pressure increases later in the project, these conflicts may be even more difficult to resolve.

A final team dynamics task is determining how the team will document its activity through the course. Students should keep track of their time and summarize it weekly. If it is a large team with a team leader who also serves as a coordinator, the team administrator should collect and summarize these activity reports and provide them to the team leader/coordinator and the instructor. During the project, these activity logs will help the team leader and the instructor monitor team activity and to facilitate action as needed to help distribute workloads more equitably. If it is a smaller team, these activity reports are developed by the team members and shared with the instructor. At the end, regardless of team size, the team leader should submit a summary activity report of total hours spent by the team on the project to the instructor. This is a useful number to document the value of the consulting engagement to the client. The value is a simple calculation of total hours multiplied by the prevailing local hourly consulting rate. See Appendix 1D for a sample activity log.

Initial client meeting

Once the student consulting team has gathered information from secondary sources, created a briefing paper, and developed questions, it is time to meet the client. Although in some circumstances, the client may have met the students if they came to a class to "sell" their consulting assignment, this section refers to the first meeting that occurs after the student team has picked/been assigned the client for a project. It is a good practice to meet with the client only after you have a reasonable understanding of the general environment in which the firm operates. Remember, as a small business/organization consultant, you are working in an environment that is constrained by the client's resource limitations and by their past practices, i.e., their way of doing things. You must keep in mind that the client is usually coping with a complex, rapidly changing environment and they may lack skilled or experienced staff to help them (Scarborough & Cornwall, 2019).

Students should dress professionally and begin this first meeting by giving the client a signed confidentiality agreement and completed group contact sheet (see Appendices 1B and 1C). The first meeting typically occurs at the client's business with just the students present, and the instructor should not attend this meeting. You are the professional consultant in the student team consulting (STC) arrangement, and if the instructor accompanies the students, the situation can be interpreted as the instructor and their helpers, and the student team is in danger of not being viewed as the professionals.

As the industry research should have been completed or substantially underway at this point, you can use some of this information to help the discussion by asking more informed questions. This should help you to get to the primary purpose of this meeting, namely, to understand the clients' needs so you can negotiate the problem definition for the project. This will be the foundation for the Letter of Engagement (LOE). After a tour of the facilities, use this opportunity to address key questions: How does the client envision this consulting assignment? What types of issues need to be addressed? What outcome does the client want? The more informed the team is, the better the LOE will fit the situation, likely resulting in fewer problems as the project continues.

Identifying the client's issues through root cause analysis

Abstract

This chapter presents tools, resources, and strategies for identifying the underlying problems your client is facing. A common error among consultants is to focus on symptoms without identifying the root cause. This could lead to wasteful use of resources and frustration. Conducting thorough, firm-level, industry and market analyses helps you pinpoint the issues you will address in the project.

Well-written consulting reports must include actionable and impactful recommendations. One of the most important aspects of the process for getting to those recommendations is problem/issue identification. Just as with most other diagnostic processes, solely treating symptoms leads to a waste of resources. Let us share a quick example. This process used here is a simple root cause analysis tool named the 5 Whys (iSixSigma). This is an important tool when conducting your client interviews. A consultant was brought in to find out why the Washington Monument was eroding at such a fast rate. During his investigation, this was the approach he took. See the following example conversation:

Consultant: *Why* do you think it is eroding quickly?
Maintenance: Because of the soap that we use to clean it.
C: *Why* are you using that soap?
M: Because it is one of the few that will remove the pigeon poop from the monument.
C: *Why* is there pigeon poop all over the monument?
M: Because they like the insects that fly around the lights.
C: *Why* are there insects around the lights?

M:	Because they are attracted by the new light bulbs.
C:	*Why* did you change the light bulbs?
M:	I don't know.
C:	Maybe you should change them back.

This is a simple illustration of the power of asking why. Do not be afraid to ask why. As you get to know your client's business, you will know which questions to ask. To become more informed about your client's internal operations and the external environmental in which they function, here are a selection of tools that you can use. Not every project will need to include an analysis with each of the tools. This section will be broken up into tools for internal analyses and external analyses.

Internal analysis

SWOT analysis

An internal analysis focuses on gathering and organizing data at the firm level. This is usually narrowly focused. The first tool is a SWOT Analysis. This tool identifies and organizes data on a firm's strengths, weakness, opportunities, and threats. SWOT analysis is a strategic planning technique valuable in tailoring actionable recommendations that can impact your client immediately (Morrison, 2014). Strengths and weaknesses focus on the internal operations that a firm can control, while opportunities and threats look external forces that the firm can mitigate and leverage. A thorough SWOT will include a matrix as seen in Table 3.1 and a more in-depth discussion of each of the components of a SWOT.

Following the SWOT matrix includes an in-depth discussion as to why you believe the items listed in the matrix are relevant to the firm. Each of the quadrants in the SWOT should include a bulleted list of the respective

Table 3.1 SWOT Matrix

	➢ Helpful to Organization	➢ Harmful to Organization
Internal	**S**trengths	**W**eaknesses
External	**O**pportunities	**T**hreats

Table 3.2 Possible Question Areas for SWOT

Strengths	*Weaknesses*
• Core competence • Strategic plan • Financial resources • Profitability • Business model • Technology • Marketing prowess • Management team	• Cost structure • Capital • Managerial skills • New product development capability • Marketing capacity • Strategic alignment of initiatives • Critical mass of products, sales, customers
Opportunities	*Threats*
• New products, markets, segments • Diversification • Technology • Demographic trends • Globalization • Collaboration partners	• Economy • Barriers to market entry • Competition • Demographic trends • Regulatory environment • Product or market lifecycles • Industry trends

strengths, weaknesses, opportunities, and threats. Table 3.2 presents some of the core areas that could be covered in the SWOT analysis.

TOWS analysis

A TOWS analysis is an extension of the SWOT analysis (MindTools, n.d.). You will use the data gathered for the SWOT to identify strategies with potential for success. The matrix presented in Table 3.3 provides a guideline for how to conduct a TOWS analysis.

Table 3.3 TOWS Matrix

	➢ Opportunities	➢ Threats
Strengths	**SO** These strategies will use strengths to maximize opportunities.	**ST** These strategies will use strengths to minimize threats.
Weaknesses	**WO** These strategies will minimize weaknesses by taking advantage of opportunities.	**WT** These strategies will minimize weaknesses and avoid threats.

This analysis allows you to match the strengths and weaknesses of your client to either minimize threats or maximize opportunities. After this analysis, you should have a list of actionable, impactful recommendations to provide to your client. Please see Appendices 2A and 2B for an example SWOT and accompanying TOWS Analyses.

SOAR analysis

The SOAR (strengths, opportunities, aspirations, and results) analysis is a tool like SWOT, but it focuses on what is known to work for a business (GroupMap, n.d.). This type of analysis results in a set of actions which are helpful in communicating and formulating your recommendations for your client. It is a great tool to explore new initiatives, develop a strategic plan, refocus, and redirect efforts. It is especially helpful in less developed organizations or firms looking to rebrand or launch a new product. You can find an example below (Table 3.4) with questions that are useful in conducting a SOAR analysis. Feel free to tailor the questions to your client and create new ones.

Table 3.4 SOAR Analysis

Strengths	**Opportunities**
• What is the firm great at doing or providing? • What are the firm's best accomplishments? • What makes the firm unique? • Does the company provide anything that is world class? • What strengths of the firm are most valuable? • What is(are) the firm's competitive advantage(s)?	• What partnerships could the firm form for success? • What market trends align well with the firm's strengths? • Are there unmet customer needs or wants that the firm could serve? • Are there stakeholders of the firm that are not fully engaged?
Aspirations	**Results**
• What are some of the visionary goals of the firm? • How do they imagine the role of the business or new product/service? • What does the firm and its members really care about? • What are some of the strategies the firm could use to realize their fullest potential?	• What should the firm measure to determine if they are on track (be careful to not include vanity metrics)? • How will they convert their vision into outcomes? • When will the firm know if they have achieved success?

7-S Framework

The 7-S framework is most often associated with the McKinsey & Co. consulting organization. However, the framework was created and published long before it was resurrected and made famous by the managing director at the time, Rajat Gupta. All seven forces in the model seen in Figure 3.1 need to be aligned if a company aims to move forward, grow, and progress. The originators of the model believed that productive organizational change is the interaction between all the 7-Ss in the framework. There are many sources online that provide a more detailed description of the framework.

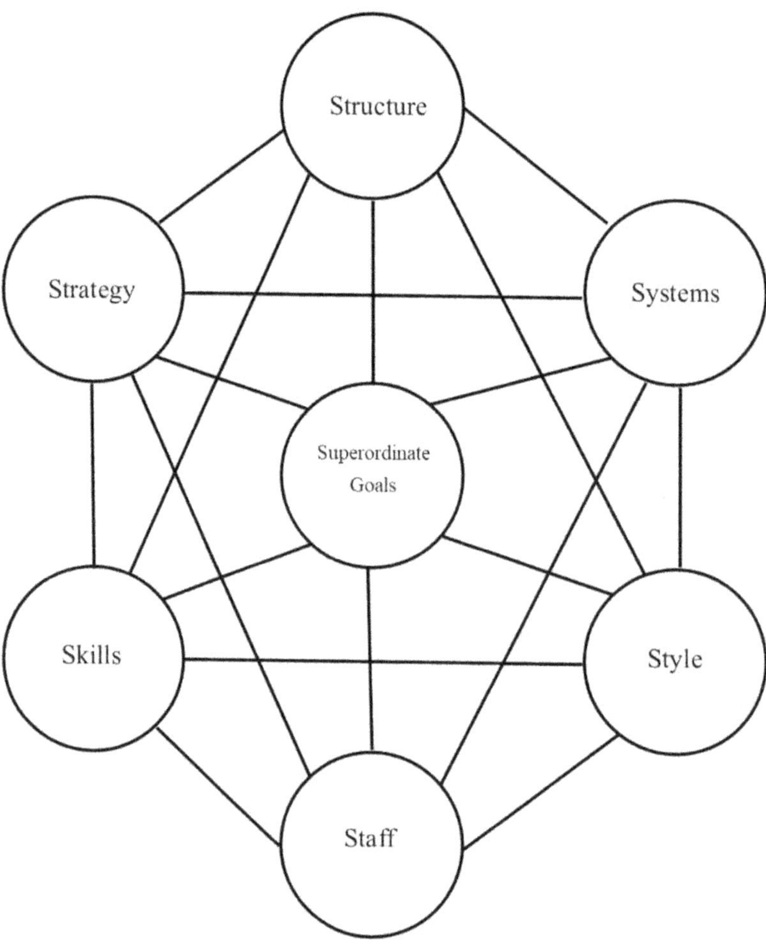

Figure 3.1 7-S framework.

Value proposition canvas

The value proposition canvas can assist your client in visualizing how their customers make decisions and, therefore, they can create value and offers that will be more appealing to them (Osterwalder, Pigneur, Bernarda, & Smith, 2014). There are two components of the canvas: the customer profile and the company's value proposition. There are great online templates that can assist you as you design the value proposition canvas for your client. The customer profile includes gains, pains, and customer jobs. The gains are the benefits customers expect and/or need; pains are the negative emotions and risks customers face; and the customer jobs are the tasks customers are attempting to perform or problems they are trying to solve. The value map allows you to organize the products and services that create gains and alleviate pains for your client's customers. Figure 3.2 demonstrates the template for the canvas.

B2B International (n.d.) takes the use of the value proposition canvas a step further. Their process ensures that the value proposition is differentiated

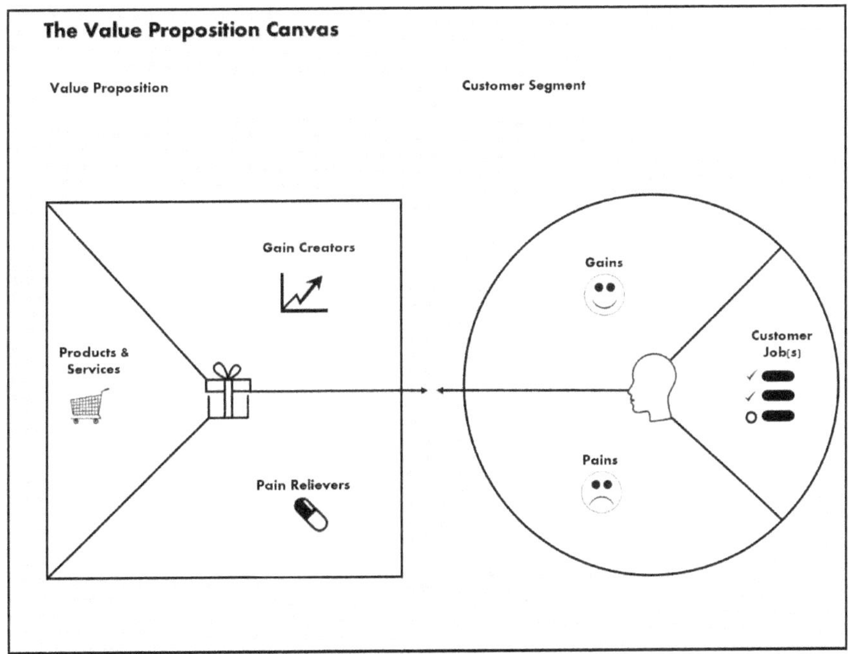

Figure 3.2 Value proposition canvas. Adapted from https://www.strategyzer.com/canvas/value-proposition-canvas

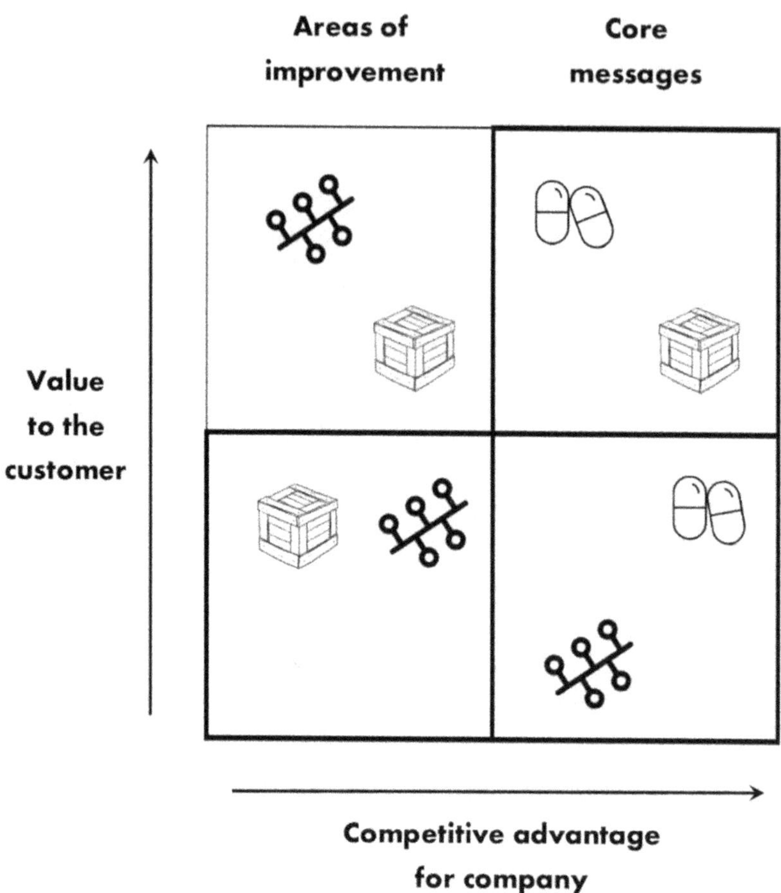

Figure 3.3 Value proposition matrix. Adapted from https://www.b2binternational.com/research/methods/faq/what-is-the-value-proposition-canvas

and describes a company's competitive advantage. Figure 3.3 presents the matrix to plot the aspects of your client's value proposition.

USP analysis

The unique selling proposition (USP) analysis is a combination of an internal and external analysis (Shewan, 2020). This tool will help you work with your client to identify their competitive advantage. The internal portion of this analysis is that they will have to reflect on their business. The external

Criterion	Your Client	Competitor #1	Competitor #2	Competitor #3

Figure 3.4 USP grid.

component is that they will have to compare those reflections against some of their top competitors. Sometimes, this approach is also called a competitive analysis. To begin this process, you must identify the top five criteria that your client competes in with its top three competitors. Therefore, you also must identify the top three competitors. Your client can provide their top three competitors, as a starting point. However, you should do further analysis as the client may be unaware of an important competitor. An example grid for this analysis can be seen in Figure 3.4. You would rank your client and the competitors on a scale from 1 to 10 with 1 being poor and 10 being great.

Then you can graph the results from the grid with the criteria on the X-axis and the score out of 10 on the Y-axis. This will provide your client with another visual highlighting how they measure up against their top competition. The final part of the USP identification process is to look at the data and come up with a USP statement. This statement will highlight the ways your client excels against the competition.

External analysis

An external analysis places your client's experience in a larger context. It is important to understand not only the factors that are directly under the control of a firm but also the environment in which they operate. This includes having a more intimate understanding of the market, industry, political environment, and technological forces that, as they change, will impact the strategic decision-making process for your client. Here are a few tools to help you build a better contextual understanding, so that you can provide your client with meaningful recommendations.

Critical success factors

Critical success factors (CSF) are strategies that are critical for your client to be successful in areas such as customer relations (Rockart, 1979). These factors are vital as you ensure your client is taking the proper strategic posture. CSF are not decided by your client but are determined by the needs and preferences of customers and the market. The process of uncovering these factors relies on research to understand what motivates customers to buy from your client. A company will usually have between three and five factors. The success factors for clients will differ based on industry, location, and target market. You can use many of the internal analysis tools to determine your client's CSF. Key success factors: address competitive forces; set direction for employee behavior and expectations; outline the requirements for a company to succeed; and provide boundaries for decision-making. As you help your client identify these factors, it will keep them from trying to be everything to everyone. One of the weaknesses of many firms is the lack of a clear identity, and it leads to inefficiencies and a lack of resiliency.

6W model

The 6W model is a tool for analyzing the external environment of a company. There are many versions of the 6W that range from SEO optimization to police investigations. This section will focus on the use of the 6W model for customer analysis. You can use this tool to investigate potential customers and study the behavior of existing customers (Ferrell & Hartline, 2016). The underlying approach for the 6W framework is the questions being asked: who, what, where, when, and why (x2). This model is a preliminary approach, and, many times, the questions cannot be answered right away by the student team or the client. However, understanding what you do not know is just as important as knowing what you do know. Table 3.5 presents the high-level six questions with example sub-questions to help you answer the top-level questions with your client. The questions in the table focus on products but could easily be applied to services, and this list of questions is not exhaustive. This is only a starting point and illustrative of the nature of the 6W framework approach.

Table 3.5 6 W Model for Customer Analysis

1. **Who** are our current and potential customers? • What are the demographic, geographic, and psychological characteristics of the customers? • Is the customer the end-user? • Who influences the purchase besides the customer?
2. **What** do our current and potential customers do with their products (value proposition)? • How much of our product do customers buy? • Is our product a complement of another product? • Do our customers use our product differently? • What is the entire lifecycle of our product?
3. **Where** do the customers purchase the product? • What is the distribution process for our product? • How heavily does product sales rely on e-commerce? • Are there international customers? • What are all the points of sale for the product?
4. **When** do the customers buy the product? • Are sales seasonal? • Do marketing promotions impact sales? • How dependent are our sales on the social and physical environments of customers?
5. **Why** does the customer buy from this organization? • What are the basic properties of our product? • Does the competition offer different properties? How do we compare? • Are the customer needs time-sensitive? Will they change? Why? How? • Are lasting relationships with customers important?
6. **Why** doesn't the customer buy from this organization? • What customer needs are not met? • Are there problems with distribution? Price? Promotion? • How can potential customers be converted to actual customers?

Adapted from https://www.toolshero.com/marketing/6w-model-of-customer-analysis/

Porter's five forces

In 1979, Professor Michael E. Porter wrote about the competitive forces that shape strategy in the *Harvard Business Review* (Porter, 1979). The forces in this paper, and in subsequent tweaks, became known as Porter's five forces and shaped the study of strategy for a generation of academics and practitioners. This tool is still relevant today in measuring and investigating the attractiveness of an industry. Table 3.6 presents the five forces and subareas that are important for adequately measuring the attractiveness of an industry

(Porter, 1998). Each of the forces can be effectively measured by low, med-low, med, med-high, and high. Gulati, Mayo, and Nohria (2017) outline an effective process for implementing the tool. Table 3.6 offers a brief take on Gulati et al.'s discussion.

Table 3.6 Porter's Five Forces

1. Threat of new entrants • Supply-side economies of scale • Demand-side benefits of scale • Customer switching costs • Capital requirements • Incumbency advantages • Unequal access to distribution channels • Restrictive government policy
2. Bargaining power of suppliers A supplier is powerful when: • the supplier industry is more concentrated than the industry it sells to. • industry participants face switching costs for changing suppliers. • no or few substitutes exist. • the supplier can threaten to forward-integrate. • the suppliers do not rely heavily on the industry.
3. Threat of substitutes • Regulatory environment • Barriers to entry • Obvious substitutes (competitor) • Non-obvious substitutes (product that satisfies the same needs)
4. Bargaining power of customers A customer group is powerful when: • the group is concentrated or purchases in large volumes. • the seller's products are undifferentiated. • buyers face switching costs. • buyers could backward-integrate.
5. Rivalry among existing competitors Intense rivalry exists when: • the product or service in the industry lacks differentiation. • there are low switching costs for buyers. • fixed costs for the firms in the industry are high and marginal costs are low. • capacity expansion must happen in large increments. • the product is perishable. • competitors are numerous or roughly equal in size and power. • industry growth is slow. • exit barriers are high.

PESTLE

The PESTLE analysis is a strategic management tool that helps identify, analyze, and monitor key external factors that could have an impact on your client (pestleanalysis.com, n.d.). This can be an expansion of the SWOT analysis presented in the internal analysis section. The factors included in the PESTLE analysis (political, economic, social, technological, legal, and environmental) can help expand on the opportunities and threats for your client. Table 3.7 presents an overview with examples and questions to complete a PESTLE analysis. The template provided in Table 3.7 offers some example questions to ask to get started with the analysis; however, you will need to add to this list based on your client.

Resources for research

Some of the suggested resources listed here are free on the web, but databases typically can only be accessed if your library has a license with them. However, many public libraries have added business information databases, so you should also check there if your institution does not subscribe to them. We recommend that you work with a business librarian. A college or university will typically have someone in the library who is responsible for supporting business research. Often, the first step in the research process is determining what code your client's business falls under.

Coding

Understanding the use of codes when researching in some databases may be useful. Here is a list of some commonly used coding systems in industry and market research banks.

Standard Occupational Classification (SOC)

These codes are commonly used by the Department of Labor and other federal agencies to classify workers into occupational categories. These categories are based on job duties, skills, and experience.

Table 3.7 PESTLE Analysis

Political	**Economic**	**Social**
What government policies can be beneficial to the firm? What government policies can be detrimental to the firm? Is the political environment stable? Are there potential regulations that could impact the firm? Some of the categories of policies and political climate to consider include: tax, trade, corruption, bureaucracy, intellectual property, environmental, labor, consumer protection, and so on.	What economic forces or trends may be beneficial to the firm? What economic forces or trends may be detrimental to the firm? How do economic fluctuations affect the firm's pricing, revenue, or costs? Some of the categories of potential economic impact include: economic growth, taxation, seasonality, interest rates, exchange rates, credit, monetary policy, commodity prices, raw material cost, unemployment rates, labor costs, immigration, and so on.	What values and beliefs impact customers' purchasing decisions? How do cultural trends affect the business? Some of the categories of attitudes and beliefs to consider include: health, value of leisure, work ethic, customer service, religion, culturally acceptable (or not) behavior, lifestyle choices, family size, perception of money, and so on.
Technological What technology innovations are on the horizon that could impact the firm? Are there technology trends which the firm could use to its benefit? Examples of technological categories to consider include: communications, customer technology access and adoption, automation, emerging technology, intellectual property, research and development, competitor technology, and so on.	**Legal** What regulations and laws directly impact the firm? Are these regulations to the benefit or detriment of the firm? What are the regulations in related markets that could impact the firm? Examples of legal factors to consider include: consumer protection, labor, health and safety, environmental, data protection, tax, discrimination, product labelling, advertising standards, antitrust, trade, and so on.	**Environmental** How does the physical environment affect the firm? What are the impacts of climate and weather on the firm? How does the firm impact the environment? Is the firm required (and on target) to meet certain environmental targets? Examples of environmental forces to consider include: carbon emissions/footprint, waste management, pollution, climate impact, weather, renewable energy, toxic chemical handling, and so on.

Standard Industrial Classification (SIC)

These six-digit codes are used to categorize business activities. The industries are grouped by a granular description of the products and services provided by firms. You can search here for SIC codes: https://www.osha.gov/pls/imis/sicsearch.html

North American Industry Classification System (NAICS)

This classification system is a cooperative effort between the United States, Mexico, and Canada to maintain classification consistency. It was intended to insure representation of emerging technologies and service industries in general. These codes can be very narrowly defined. You can discover the proper code by searching here for NAICS: https://www.census.gov/eos/www/naics/

United States International Trade Commission

This is an independent, federal agency that produces trade policy advice to the U.S. government. They maintain the Harmonized Tariff Schedule which produces a set of codes for imports (HTS) and exports (HS). The United Nations also has its own coding system (SITC).

Databases and sources

ABI/INFORM

First Research Industry Profiles are available in this database, and these profiles are unique in that they also provide specific information for someone working with the decision-makers in this industry. What are some specific issues for the chief executive officer or what is the main focus for the chief financial officer? In addition, the "Call Prep Questions" provided are useful in problem identification.

American FactFinder

American FactFinder is the source for population, housing, economic, and geographic information. Community facts are available by simply typing in a location. You can also run guided and advanced searches, pulling data from thousands of reports pages.

AnnualReports.com

AnnualReports.com is just what it sounds like, a free link to many annual reports.

BizMiner

BizMiner is a subscription-based database typically available through university libraries and provides financial and market analysis on over 9,000 industries.

BLS Industries at a Glance

The Bureau of Labor Statistics (BLS) includes workforce current and projected numbers for over 100 industries and sectors.

Business Source Complete

The database full-text content includes financial data, case studies, industry reports, market research reports, country reports, and company profiles.

Business Source Premier

This source includes access to domestic and international MarketLine industry profiles. These industry profiles are data-intensive with limited written analysis.

CareerOneStop

This is a government site that helps connect you with job information in several ways. Like the BLS information, it is concerned with workforce statistics, but it also allows you to go to local levels.

Census Business Builder: Small Business Edition

If you are considering recommending a new location or an expansion to a new location, the Census Business Builder is a suite of services that provides selected demographic and economic data from the Census Bureau tailored to specific types of users. You pick your location, and then select the type of information you want about the site: possible competitors, income, housing characteristics, and so on. There are tutorials for using the Business Builder at the website.

Consumer Expenditure Survey

This resource lists the latest annual purchases of Americans, divided by age, gender, race, and income level. It is also available for sectors of the country and includes some analysis of the data on the site, as well as the data themselves.

Data Axle

This tool provides instant and real-time access to accurate in-depth information on 16 million U.S. businesses and 184 million U.S. households.

Editor and Publisher Market Guide

Market data for more than 1,600 cities and all 3,096 counties. Projects retail sales by broad category. Includes income levels, disposable income, and some retail projections.

esri Tapestry Segmentation

Tapestry gives you insights to help you identify your best customers, optimal sites, and underserved markets. Tapestry Segmentation classifies neighborhoods into 67 unique segments based not only on demographics but also socioeconomic characteristics.

Euromonitor International

Provides integrated access to statistics, reports, insightful comments, and business information sources. Euromonitor creates global reports for Western Europe, Eastern Europe, North America, Latin America, Asia Pacific, Oceania, Africa, and the Middle East.

GlobalEdge

Michigan State University has developed a substantial resource for business information, particularly for international business, and industry reports (https://globaledge.msu.edu/).

Google advanced search

Google has become synonymous with searching. Though this can be a powerful tool, there are a few tips which will help make your searches relevant and provide access to credible data. However, as with any research project, be sure to understand where the data you use come from, how they were collected, and for what purpose they were was intended to be used.

IBISWorld

IBISWorld is a provider of industry research reports on over 700 U.S. industries. Use this database to search by NAICS codes, keywords, or industries. IBIS also publishes several specialized industry reports that focus on niche and emerging industries.

LexisNexis Academic

LexisNexis is a news and legal database where you can search for company, executive, statutory, and case law information on a local, state, and federal level. However, some of the information is based on surveys answers and therefore is not very specific.

Mediaweek Marketer's Guide to Media

Includes trends and demographics for media with separate sections on men, women, adults, teens, and Hispanics.

Mintel Reports: USA

Research reports covering European, UK-specific, and US consumer markets. Results will be market, rather than industry, driven. You can generate reports to analyze market drivers, sizes, trends, market segmentation, and data on consumer attitudes and purchasing habits.

ProQuest

This platform contains multiple databases for business research. A simple online search will provide more information about the databases and the type of data accessible. Here are some of the databases included in ProQuest.

- Hoover's Company Profiles – includes over 40,000 public and non-public companies globally.

- OxResearch – find articles from Oxford and other university think-tanks.
- Snapshots – find market research overviews on 40+ industries.
- ABI/Inform Trade & Industry – in-depth coverage of companies, products, and executives.
- ProQuest Entrepreneurship
- ProQuest Statistical Insight

QuickFacts

QuickFacts provides statistics for all states and counties, and all cities and towns with a population of 5,000 or more. You can run side-by-side comparisons for up to six locations simultaneously (www.census.gov/quickfacts/fact/table/US/PST045219).

Securities Exchange Commission

The Securities Exchange Commission has annual reports and other documents available for searching (https://www.sec.gov/edgar/searchedgar/companysearch.html).

Simply Analytics

Simple, step-by-step instructions for creating maps using pre-loaded statistics. Options include demographics, consumer buying patterns, types and numbers of establishments, ethnicity and age variables.

Standard & Poor's (S&P) NetAdvantage

NetAdvantage has over 50 industry profiles. Click on the "Industries" button on the top bar to access the drop-down menu of choices. The S&P industry profiles are also available historically. Choose the profile first and then access the date drop-down menu. While the main profiles are U.S.-centric, there are global profiles available for Asia, Europe, and Latin America.

Statista

A portal for statistics for market research, especially in consumer and emerging markets. This is data collected and shared between shareholders such as Proctor & Gamble or General Motors. The information is available with attribution and is delivered in presentation and infographic formats.

The U.S. Census Bureau

The U.S. Census Bureau is the definitive source for all things demographic and statistical in the United States. The data collected by the Census are accessed through this portal. This will give you a good opportunity to use the NAICS code(s) you identified (https://www.census.gov/).

ThomasNet

This is a free, open access source. You can find research and data on over 700,000 commercial and industrial suppliers (https://www.thomasnet.com).

Trade Associations and Publications

For every industry, there is an association or trade group. This is an organization that will collect information through surveys and analysis, create position papers on industry-specific legal and governmental issues, and lobby for the industry. Much of the information created by an association is kept private for the members, but some associations share a great deal of good data with the public. The easiest way to identify the association for your client is to ask them, or you can also search online for your industry name and the word 'association'.

Another great source of up-to-date information are trade publications, such as trade journals or newsletters. These are publications that are created for people who are involved in the industry currently, rather than academic scholars. Some are available on the association's website, but many are only available through one of the business databases, such as Business Source Premier, ABI/INFORM, or LexisNexis.

Client contract development and relationship management

Abstract

This chapter will cover the client contract and the relationship aspects of a consulting project, beginning with letter of engagement, project management, and project communications.

Letter of engagement

As mentioned, clients may or may not have a good grasp of their needs. They may be focusing on the symptoms of a problem but not the underlying cause. The issue may also be complex, and the client may not be able to articulate it correctly. Thus, it is important to probe deeply to develop a clear understanding of their circumstances, with the goal of creating clarity in the Letter of Engagement (LOE). Creating clarity is essential for an effective consulting project with a small firm/organization (Porth & Salthis, 1998). It is imperative that ambiguity be as limited as possible regarding:

1. The project objective(s) – what does the team intend to do?
2. The approach – how does the team intend to do it? With what milestones happening at what points in time?
3. The deliverables – what will the client receive from the project?

The problem definition comes from a clear understanding of the client's needs. The LOE identifies what you are going to do, why, and by when. It provides all parties with a clear statement of the outcomes of this problem-based learning (PBL) activity (Peterson, 2004). What needs to be researched? What issues must be resolved?

In contrast, the approach is the methodology question. How does the team intend to meet the objectives? The team needs to be specific as to how they will accomplish the objectives. What are their tactics? Since all projects normally have a secondary research component, what will that entail? What sources will be used? Will the team be conducting primary research? If so, what type (interview, survey, observation), and what are the details of that research process?

Clarity of the approach increases the client's confidence that your team knows how to successfully complete the project. It also allows the client, instructor, and team to anticipate any issues that might arise during the project.

The third element in the LOE, deliverables, tells the client what will be received from the team. The instructor and the client are expecting the team to produce the deliverables in the LOE and anything missing is a problem. It is better to have a shorter list of outcomes and have them fully executed than a much longer list that cannot be completed.

Thus, a note of caution. Student consulting contracts often tend to promise more than can be delivered or tend to be less specific than they should be. Therefore, different expectations as to what is a quality product might result from a vaguely worded LOE. In other words, a high-quality engagement that is narrowly defined is better than a project that addresses too many areas and results in shallow findings. In a student consulting engagement, more resources (people or time) cannot usually be added to the project to offset an "over-promised" LOE, as the semester will end and there are no extra students who can pitch in. Quality, not quantity, is crucial. The deliverables will be provided to the client in two ways – in a final written report and a presentation. Appendix 2E provides an LOE example.

In addition, there are usually three levels that your team must be concerned with when developing the LOE. Somewhat larger firms/organizations tend to have more complex administrative structures and more people who may be affected by the implementation of the team's recommendations. Therefore, you should consider the following issues:

1. How to deal with the client's definition of the problem – the client may be describing symptoms instead of the root cause(s) or having difficulty articulating the problem. How do you handle the situation if you disagree with the client's assessment?

2. How to deal with the underlying organizational issues that may have caused the problem – these are situations where the firm's structure contributes to the problem?
3. How to handle any politics of the situation – who might be affected by your proposed changes? How do you get buy-in? Is the situation workable?

A last issue to consider in the LOE is reimbursement to the students for out-of-pocket expenses. Costs that are expected to occur during a project should be the client's responsibility. Your instructor may ask you to prepare a pro-forma budget proposal for client approval and to include a summary of that budget in the LOE. Typical expenses might be travel, parking, telephone, and/or duplication/binding cost. To the extent that much of the research may be secondary, there may be little or no cost. In some cases, the client has paid a participation fee to the school, and normal expenses may be covered under that fee. However, since potential expenses are often unknown at the beginning of a consulting engagement, typical language in an LOE budget request could simply suggest a spending limit and require client approval before any monies are expended above that limit or for any special purchases related to the consulting engagement. If there is a budget in the LOE, then the team's treasurer is responsible for it.

Project management

Once the LOE has been finalized by the client, student team, and instructor, it is time to implement the plan. Your team should have developed a general map of the project in the LOE, one that uses a project management process (see the LOE in Appendix 2E). This allows tasks to be broken down into specific action steps, with beginning and ending dates for each step, and the student(s) responsible for that step. For example, if primary research is the methodology and the team is surveying a student population at a college for dining preferences (i.e., if the client was a food service provider), some specific action steps might include:

- Identify the student body parameters (commuters only, on-campus only, full-time or part-time, etc.)
- Develop a mechanism to reach the sample population (campus mail, intercept interview techniques, etc.)
- Design a survey instrument (with assistance from instructor)

- Gain client approval of the survey design
- Conduct a pilot test of survey on student sample (if time permits)
- Revise and edit the survey based on the pilot test results (if pilot was done)
- Administer the survey
- Conduct data entry of survey returns
- Analyze the data
- Develop findings from the data

Most of the student population survey research listed above has additional steps. For example, survey design has additional actions such as topic selection, survey length, specific question structure, and so on. If primary research is not the best methodology for the project, then a secondary research protocol is used. This typically includes internet exploration, database searches, company research, and so on, preferably under the guidance of the business librarian as discussed earlier in the industry analysis.

The point here is to break down the project into discrete steps with a start/completion date. Furthermore, the larger the number of team members, the more important it is to break down the project into this level of detail as coordination among larger teams is very critical.

The nature of a student team consulting project requires a disciplined, time-management approach throughout the semester. There will likely be other issues that will arise, outside of the team's control, which can cause delays. One example of an unavoidable situation occurred when Hurricane Sandy struck the east coast. A student team working with a client had a major delay when the client lost power for two weeks and was unable to respond to the students' requests. This occurred during the last month of the engagement. If the students were procrastinating (which they were not), the project could have easily carried over into the spring semester, causing all types of logistical problems. Hence, there is no room in a student consulting program for intentionally operating like a "one-week wonder," i.e. delaying work on the project until near the end of the semester and then pulling all-nighters and so on to finish. The use of a project management approach helps keep the team on track.

Project communication

As the project takes shape, there are several key issues that will emerge. Among the first is instructor/team communication. Your team needs to regularly keep your instructor informed of their activities occurring outside the classroom. One way to do this is with the progress report. In this report, there can be sections to describe the team's output and each individual student's activities. This allows the instructor to monitor individual's contributions to the team effort. A typical use of the report is for it to be submitted approximately two days ahead of the next instructor/team meeting. This allows the instructor to research any issues the team has raised before the meeting and be able to offer solutions. Progress reports should be made by the designated team member to the instructor, typically on a weekly basis and can be submitted electronically. See Appendix 2C for a sample example of a completed progress report.

Teams often have a standard meeting time with the instructor. At these meetings, your team needs to be prepared to discuss project execution, possible scheduling glitches, and any other problems. Problems should be caught early. The progress report also gives the instructor insight into potential issues, so students need to be ready to discuss possible solutions. Proper project management can provide the structure needed to let the students know if they are on track. Another important tool is the weekly activity log, a summary of the week's hours spent by the students. This activity log helps the instructor monitor student activity and take corrective action, especially if it appears that the students' efforts are unbalanced or that teams are spending either more or less time on the project than anticipated. Although the efficiency of teams can vary so that some teams may spend less time to complete the project than others, projects are being done for academic credit and the work should reflect the time you would anticipate being spent on a typical class. These time summaries should be expressed in incremental hours for the week as well as cumulative hours for the engagement. As mentioned earlier, at the end of the project, the team can multiply its total project hours by the prevailing local hourly consulting rate so the instructor can give the client an indication of the comparable value received from the student consulting team.

Clients, too, need progress updates. The nature and frequency of these updates is typically defined in the LOE, as fieldwork assignments can vary greatly in scope and duration. The team and the client are encouraged to develop their own reporting arrangements. In addition to whatever progress updates the team and client choose to adopt, there are generally two formal client reports. The first of these is the LOE. This can be signed and emailed, mailed, or delivered to the client face-to-face. The second formal report is the final presentation itself. Additional comments on the final report will be found later in the text.

Occasionally, a client may not be responsive to the students. If this occurs early, it can be an indicator of how the project will go. One solution in these circumstances may be for the instructor to replace the unresponsive client with another one. Fortunately, these glitches are relatively rare since most clients are very responsive to the team's needs. After all, your goal is to help the client's business.

Another issue that may arise with the client is a lack of cooperation regarding data access. In a student consulting engagement, it is expected that the client will provide needed information to the team in a timely manner. During a typical semester, there is no extra time to wait for the client to provide data. A delay is costly if a team must scramble to make up for lost time. Therefore, what should you do if the client fails to provide needed information to the team?

First, notify the instructor. The instructor and team then determine how to handle the situation. The second step is to proceed with as much of the project as can be done without the data, in the hope that the information will be forthcoming. If the issue persists, the third step is to adjust the project parameters so client data are not necessary to complete the project. This needs to be done only with the permission and assistance of the instructor and in consultation with the client.

Another issue that may arise is that the client may not be able to articulate their needs correctly. This can be a problem as you will be relying on information provided by the client to help identify issues and to provide background data. The client has been involved in the industry and usually is a valuable resource. However, it is important to get independent verification of information, where possible, so the student team can work with as reasonable and accurate information as possible. This may be from the business librarian, other employees of the client, others in the industry, and so on. You may find that you cannot verify the information, but you should always try.

The last issue in this section is that there may be different expectations between the client and the team as to the scope of the project, due to the ambiguous nature of a consulting assignment. This is called scope creep. Scope creep occurs where the client believes the team will be working on a certain set of activities and that those activities keep expanding due to the fluid nature of a consulting assignment. As the project continues, peripheral issues may be uncovered which the client feels should also be addressed. Meanwhile, the team is operating on the original set of assumptions. If this occurs, you need to immediately communicate with the instructor and the client as the project evolves. The key is having clarity in what is to be done and that occurs in a clearly delineated letter of engagement (LOE), discussed earlier, which is the contract negotiated between the team and the client at the beginning of the engagement. It helps prevent confusion about what will be done and should describe how any changes in the scope of work will be handled.

Although consulting programs will vary at different schools, there is usually no formal interim report because there often are no interim results. The student team is usually still exploring different avenues and any reports could be misleading to the client. Informal reporting mechanisms, often tied to requests for information from the clients, can keep the client informed without committing the team to a specific direction too early in the project.

Based on the LOE and its project management timeline, the project may be broken down into draft sections of the final report. You and your instructor should find it mutually beneficial to utilize evaluative feedback loops based on the draft report submissions (homework). You have an opportunity to finalize the final report with the knowledge that a large portion of your project has received written feedback from the instructor. Homework assignments can be the LOE and at least two sections of the final report, plus any other sections deemed appropriate by the instructor. The client should not see these homework sections. If the student team has missed the mark, they will likely have to redo the homework section, and a client should never see this kind of output from the team. You want to be perceived as professionals and, therefore, the client should only see a finished, polished product.

At the conclusion of the engagement, you will prepare your final written report and presentation for the client. Once a set of tentative conclusions and recommendations have been drafted, it is time to ask the "so what" question. You need to rigorously question the report's findings for relevance – what is important, why is it important, how will implementing this report's findings improve the situation of the client? Why does it matter? There must be a clear enough answer to the "so what" question for the final report and presentation to be meaningful to the client. According to Porth and Saltis (1998), the team needs to realize that:

> Organizations need customized solutions tailored to the unique circumstances and resource capability of the firm. Standardized and one-size-fits-all answers that may work in a larger firm environment

> can be useless to the small business if they do not have the resources to pull it off. Solutions that are relatively simple, easy to implement, and inexpensive will more likely be implemented.
>
> (p. 16)

Two capabilities are needed to develop good solutions to a problem(s). The first is creativity to generate several effective alternatives. This happens with an attitude of inquiry, i.e. keeping an open mind. The second is decision-making. Later in the project, you will decide which option best fits the client's situation and advocate for that choice. Knowing when to make this switch can be a challenge due to the level of uncertainty in the consulting process, and why consulting is often called "managing ambiguity."

5 Project deliverables

Abstract

The focus of this chapter is to ensure you can extract the relevant information and data from your previous analyses and develop actionable recommendations for your client. Guidance is provided for the written report and final presentation.

Final report

The flow of the report should build upon the sections turned in earlier for feedback, which are now finalized. Each report's content and structure will depend on the nature of the consulting engagement as depicted in the letter of engagement (LOE). Each consulting situation is unique, but the basic outline of the final report will include an internal analysis, an external analysis, recommendations, and appendices. See Appendices 2F and 2G for examples of final reports.

An internal analysis may include a background of the company and a firm-level analysis. Refer to Chapter 3 for a list of possible tools to use to conduct this type of analysis. This type of analysis will typically combine primary and secondary data. Some examples include SWOT, TOWS, SOAR, 7-S, and Unique Selling Proposition. Factors to consider in this section are business structure, product offerings, equipment/facilities, operational policies/procedures, marketing, social media tactics, pricing strategies, logistics/distribution, finance, and business strategy. See the example reports and example SWOT and TOWS analysis in the Appendices 2A and 2B.

An external analysis provides the context in which your client operates. These often include market- and industry-level analysis. Refer to Chapter 3 for a list of possible tools to use to conduct these types of analyses and for resources to find secondary data. Some example approaches to use include Key Success Factors, 6W, Porter's Five Forces, and PESTLE. Factors to consider in this section are industry and market trends, market size and growth projections, critical success factors, technology, and legal, political, and environmental factors. See the analyses provided in the example reports in Appendices 2F and 2G.

Once you have researched the problem(s), come up with options, and developed your preferred solution for the client, you may think that the report is done. However, one key area left to focus on is an implementation schedule. This section is created as one of the last parts of the report because you cannot develop a schedule until you have decided on your recommendation(s). Selecting an appropriate timeframe for the implementation of your recommendations can be tricky. Ultimately, it is the client's choice as to what to adopt and how quickly. You have a better chance of the client following your recommendations if your implementation schedule is realistic, given the resource constraints of your client.

Well-written recommendations must be concise, specific, and actionable. One tip to make sure they are concise is to avoid the use of prepositions when possible. Leading with an action verb leads to a more actionable recommendation. Please see Appendix 1E for a list of action verbs. This list is not exhaustive, but it provides commonly used examples. An example of a non-specific recommendation would be "Have a Marketing Plan," which leaves more questions than provides answers or guidance for the client. A more specific recommendation statement would be "Implement a Social Media Ambassador Campaign."

This is the bread and butter of your report, and this is your place to show that you have something of value to offer to the client. Be confident and maintain a professional tone. Your focus here should be on answering the questions what, why, and how for each recommendation. Answering the question "what" is done by writing a concise, specific, and actionable recommendation statement. The "why" will come from the text, outside reading, case studies, and so on, and you should use citations to strengthen your argument. Examples of companies that have implemented similar recommendations and seen success are very helpful in clearly demonstrating the importance of your recommendation.

The final component of the recommendation section addresses "how" your client implements your suggestions. Implementation plays a substantial role in creating value by providing a plan for action. It provides the details for resource allocation, time commitment, prioritization, and the necessary steps for implementation. A critical objective in this process is to provide your client with a report that allows them to make impactful changes and improve decision-making within the organization. This requires focusing on answering these three important questions in the recommendation section. See the recommendation section provided in the example reports in Appendices 2F and 2G.

The report should be professional in appearance. Your team will provide a final report for review/grading prior to presenting it to the client. After this review, and at the final presentation, the instructor and each representative of the client should receive a final copy. Finally, an important and collegial closure to the project is a formal thank you note from the team to the client. The note can be most effective if it is given as the final activity of the meeting and provided separately from the written report. Although you will likely know what you want to say, an example can be found in Appendix 2D.

Final presentation

Much like your final report, the client presentation should focus on the recommendations. Delivering the presentation is a very important part of the learning process. As such, everyone should participate. It also provides your client with a final opportunity to interact with the team and ask any pressing questions. The purpose of this section is to help you understand expectations for the presentation and provide some best practices.

One effective presentation style is for the team leader to tell the client what they are going to hear and then come back to wrap it up (tell them what they heard) after the other students have presented their sections. You need decide if the client should ask questions during the presentation or hold them until the end. Holding until the end typically allows for a better flow. All students should have a speaking role at the presentation, as it is an important part of the evaluation process (see next section), but they do not have to have equal time presenting. There may be some members of your team who are better at presenting and you might want to maximize those skills. You should seek your instructor's guidance on this issue.

The length can vary based on the complexity of the project and the number of students on the team, but a typical presentation time is about an hour, including time for questions and answers. You should dress professionally. The presentation could happen on campus, at your client's location, or virtually. If conducted in person, this provides an excellent opportunity for a photo or video shoot. Pictures can then be posted on the web or on social media and sent to other media outlets, but only after consent from your client. The school and your client can gain excellent publicity from these outreach efforts, and the students can use these materials as evidence of their professional work. A screenshot during a virtual presentation can also be used, with the consent of the client.

You should practice the presentation to check on timing, flow, and content. If there is a mentor working with the team, then the mentor should view the presentation and provide feedback. The instructor may also be involved, or it may be done with the mentor only. If there is no mentor, this practice should be done with your instructor so that feedback can be offered. It also affords the chance to see if the "what," "why," and "how" questions are adequately addressed. At the presentation, you will give the client the finished report. Doing so in the beginning allows the client to follow along with the presentation and may make it easier to explain some sections. However, there is a risk that the client will start reading the report and not focus on the presentation. Giving the report at the end of the presentation solves that attention issue. This is a choice that should be discussed with your instructor and team, as both ways can have their good/bad points. Below are guidelines, best practices, and common mistakes from these types of student presentations:

Guidelines

- ~ 60 minutes (including Q&A)
- Professional dress
- Provide client with parking pass (if campus based)
- Escort client to presentation room (if campus based)
- Allow adequate travel time (if off campus)
- Determine accessible technology (if off campus)
- Have water and a pen to offer the client
- Bring a printed copy of the report for each client representative (email a Word version to the client lead)

Best practices

- Create an agenda for the presentation and distribute to all attendees
- Assign someone within the team to facilitate the presentation

- Lead with thanking the client on behalf of everyone (give names)
- Let the client know the format for Q&A
  - Wait till the end
  - Open conversation
  - After each set of recommendations
- Determine if your instructor prefers slides or not. If you use slides, keep them simple (slides are needed if you have technical information to show [or complex data])
- As you present, think about having a conversation with the client
  - Tell stories about your visits/interviews and use this as support for your key points
  - Relate the client's stories to material from other sources
- Do not attack the client or their processes
- Keep a helpful tone
- Encourage the client to take notes
- Make sure the client is aware of the assumptions of your consulting team
- Give credit to and include your team members
- Provide cues and transitions when switching presenters

Most common mistakes

- Not practicing multiple times as a team
- Rushing or rapid pace
- Using "ums" frequently
- Assuming the client knows what you are talking about
- Only knowing your section of the report and presentation (particularly in a virtual environment)

In some instances, final presentations must be completed in a virtual environment. Many of the guidelines, best practices, and common mistakes mentioned above remain relevant to a virtual presentation. However, there are additional factors to consider ensuring an effective presentation. Below are additional factors to consider.

Virtual factors

- Be cognizant of your background
- Use a headset and microphone
- Practice inviting guests on the virtual presentation platform (Teams, Zoom, WebEx, etc.)

- Look at the camera when you speak
- Plan who will share the screen (but have a backup or two)
- Mute when not speaking (and unmute when speaking)
- Do not be working on other tabs or documents during presentation
- Develop contingency plan in case of technical difficulties
- Use calendar invites with instructions for joining

Evaluations

One of the last activities is the evaluation. This step in the process model can consist of various evaluations designed to provide feedback to students and instructor. Feedback is important because this may be your first field-work experience. As a result, you may develop insights that will help you to improve your interpersonal skills and abilities. Feedback is important to the instructor because it helps in a continuous improvement process. The instructor can assess the responses as to what worked and what did not as an aid to improving the consulting experience in the future. Evaluations also provide data to the instructor to help calculate grades, although weights for various types of evaluations can vary substantially. There are multiple basic types of evaluations discussed here: peer, client, and instructor (team and individual). Not every consulting program will use all evaluations. It should be noted that these evaluations are not the institution's regular course evaluation that you would fill out at the end of the semester for all courses that you are taking. These four are separate evaluations that are used in the student team consulting process.

Peer evaluation – the most common formal evaluation is the peer assessment (see Appendix 1G). Sometimes during the course, and always at the conclusion of the consulting project, you will evaluate your team members and typically yourself. The key to this evaluation is to focus on the behavior of your team member during the project and not on their personality. Some team members may not get along with other members, and it is easy to rate those individuals unfavorably. Focusing on behaviors can help separate performance from personality and overcome that bias.

These evaluations should be confidential and anonymous and are used by the instructor to compute part of your grade. Since most of the consulting assignment is team based, a substantial percentage of grading points may be based on team output. The peer evaluation helps the instructor measure your individual performance in a group setting. Furthermore, as there may be a concern with any "free riders," a peer evaluation can help your individual grade better reflect your efforts and results. Peer evaluations can also be useful for self-improvement if there is a consensus among the team that a student has a deficiency in an area. This can be helpful if a peer evaluation also occurs during the semester and not just at the end, as a mid-term course correction could occur. The instructor can then share the team's concerns in the aggregate with the affected student and not identify specific comments from the peer evaluations. The confidential nature of this evaluation must be protected if honest responses are desired. In addition, even if a peer evaluation is done only at the end of the term, the feedback can still help the student in future endeavors.

Client's evaluation – this formal report allows the client to evaluate the performance of the consulting team. It usually involves completing a rating form, which assesses the final report, the presentation, and the overall performance of the consulting team. The comments are generally used to help the instructor understand the team's performance from the client's perspective. The team rating may be used by the instructor for computing your grade. Although a client may get to know some members of the team well enough to provide specific comments about individuals, generally this feedback applies only to the entire team. This is also a very common evaluation. How this feedback is used in an instructor's grading procedures will vary based on the instructor. As noted earlier, the instructor can also use client observations to improve the consulting experience for future engagements.

Instructor's evaluation – in this evaluation, the team and individual are assessed on performance directly by the instructor. This evaluation is an ongoing process that occurs through homework assignments, progress reports, and outcomes of team/instructor meetings, as well as by grades on the presentation and final written report. In addition, unlike the client evaluation, this feedback can be timely so that the team can make corrections during the consulting engagement.

There are generally two elements when evaluating team performance. First, the team is assessed on the deliverables that it produces throughout the semester. This is often based on assignments, the final written report, and the final presentation. Second, consideration is given to the team dynamics, the team's process for handling issues, and its ability to improve the team's processes. This part of the assessment is subjective, but very important, and you need to focus on communicating effectively with the instructor, client, and each other.

Finally, if there is a mentor working with team, the mentor can provide feedback on how the students have been performing. The mentor has the benefit of working with the team for the entire project and can put a context to a student's perceived performance. This is particularly useful if other evaluations provide conflicting evidence. These appraisals, along with the peer evaluation, becomes the individual student assessment in the grading system. This feedback may be shared with the student during the course. If the feedback is shared early enough in the course, it allows students to make corrections during the semester. End-of-project feedback shifts this emphasis to helping the student be better prepared for future experiences.

Professional development and conclusion

Abstract

Client-based projects can lead to positive outcomes for both students and participating organizations. From the student perspective, some of the key areas of enhancement include analytical, problem-solving, and communication skills. These experiences can often lead to additional engagement opportunities and career development. Students should feature these experiences prominently on their resumes and professional interviews.

Professional development

The previous chapters provided the framework and detailed guidance on how to be successful in complex problem-based learning courses, specifically ones featuring client-based projects. One of your primary roles during this process is to learn valuable knowledge about business research, problem identification, and how to develop viable recommendations for your client. As you learn through this experience, a second key role is to provide a value-added product for your client. Depending on the course objectives, your final report will likely include a client profile, industry, and market research, along with cost-effective recommendations and an implementation plan.

These outcomes are mutually beneficial for both you and your client and can have a lasting impact on both groups. The experiences provided by these projects combined with the skill development opportunities can benefit you as you prepare for a career after college, regardless of your workplace choice. This purpose of this chapter is to help you better understand the professional development that results from such opportunities.

Regarding your client, the work you completed this semester can provide valuable feedback from an objective outside team, as well as new methods, processes, or ideas that help them overcome critical challenges. You have been involved in a unique educational opportunity that can have a lasting impact on a "real" organization in your community. An element in the mission of many universities is to provide impactful service to their local communities, and this course has allowed you to have an active role in that process. These clients often lack the resources to hire professional consulting firms, so your service fulfills an important need. Furthermore, the success of these businesses/organizations is often directly linked to the vitality of the local community.

As a student, the benefits of this experience can extend far beyond the confines of one semester. As discussed throughout the book, there are numerous opportunities to learn important professional skills during the consulting project. These real-world experiences can enhance your resume and prepare you for career opportunities immediately after graduation.

Consulting projects provide unique opportunities to further develop your analytical and problem-solving abilities and build professional writing and communication skills. These are often cited as critical skills for young professionals as they enter the workplace. As you have learned, client reports require specialized research and thorough analysis that leads to an in-depth understanding of your client's most pressing business problems. Only after you get to that point are you then able to create viable recommendations and a tailored implementation plan.

Communication skills have also been emphasized throughout this course. The use of multiple drafts allows students to craft the report in a more cohesive manner that demonstrates value to the client. In addition, a well-written report makes it much easier for a client to understand specific recommendations and how to best implement these plans. Multiple client interactions occur during the semester and can include, but not limited to, face-to-face meetings, extended video calls, and email exchanges. In each instance, the student team must have an organized approach and display professionalism to ensure the client's trust and cooperation. These opportunities simulate the types of presentations that often occur in a business environment and help you build critical communication skills and confidence that you can be successful in the workplace.

Students also benefit from an opportunity to work within a team to complete these projects. This requires a willingness to understand team roles and dynamics and to learn how to effectively blend available resources and talents to achieve course goals. It also requires a commitment to diversity and a willingness to consider alternative points of view that allows for consensus-building to finalize a professional consulting report and client presentation.

Another important outcome of this course is the opportunity to learn the elements of the consulting process and how it all fits together. This knowledge will help you in many different professional situations and increase your marketability to prospective employers. It is also very useful for anyone who decides to pursue entrepreneurial endeavors in their career path. The ability to analyze a situation, identify problems, and then resolve these problems is a benefit that will serve you long after graduation.

Because of the skill development opportunities in these types of courses, it is encouraged that students prominently highlight these experiences on their resume. Employers are searching for prospective employees who can add value and work well within the framework of a team to achieve organizational goals. There are numerous skills you will learn and practice during your consulting projects and can be added to your resume, including industry research, teamwork effectiveness, strategic analysis, recommendation development, and implementation planning. Also, as mentioned above, there are also ample opportunities for professional communications, both written and verbal, which are often cited by employers as much-needed skills by recent graduates.

Involvement in these types of experiential learning courses serves as a springboard for additional opportunities. This can include internships with other organizations or enrollment in other client-based courses or independent studies. The skills enhanced through your consulting experience prepare you to become an attractive candidate for these prospects.

In the modern workplace, employers are looking to identify talents who can provide immediate value to their organizations. They are interested in students who are comfortable in an ambiguous environment. The ability to effectively navigate through various elements of a highly engaged consulting experience provides a unique perspective, one that is attractive to potential employers. The strategic skills gained from these projects can be the very thing that separates you from other applicants and gives you an early advantage in the workplace. Showcasing these skills allows organizations to have confidence in your ability to replicate success in comparable situations.

There are also various external competitions and other types of recognitions often linked with courses featuring client-based consulting projects.

Universities may choose to have campus-based competitions between student teams in designated courses. In addition, there are national competitions that feature these types of projects. One such competition is the Small Business Institute® Project-of-the-Year competition. This annual competition, first started in the 1980s, features the best projects from various programs across the country at both the undergraduate and graduate levels. The recognition of being selected to participate, and potentially win, competitions is an enticing element of being involved in these types of courses and can serve as a motivating factor to do your best in creating a highly impactful final report. This can also serve as another highlight for your resume and a valuable talking point in interviews with prospective employers.

The benefits gained from these experiences are why many universities are pushing more highly engaging problem-based learning courses in academic programs. Programs that demonstrate student proficiency and learning are often the most attractive. They also often lead to higher levels of student participation and overall course satisfaction. Likewise, employers are also searching for new talent with these types of experiences on their resume. And, when the course involves local clients, this serves to enhance your learning experience and provide a valuable service to the business community. So, as you conclude the semester, be sure to fully capture all aspects of the course and feature it prominently on your resume so you can reap all the benefits as you enter the professional business world.

Conclusion

The rapid growth of experiential learning has increased the opportunities to work on consulting projects with local organizations to help them resolve critical challenges. Many faculty members in business/other schools have redesigned existing courses and developed new ones focused on working with organizations/businesses in their regional community. These types of highly engaged experiences provide a rich learning environment for students and help them apply knowledge learned during their academic programs.

Consulting courses involve multiple stakeholders, so it is imperative to follow a proven framework to ensure a mutually beneficial relationship between students and participating clients. This book provides a comprehensive process that addresses key issues, such as client selection and management, team formation and dynamics, and project deliverables. In addition, commonly used research tools and relevant example reports are provided to help you better understand expectations. These chapters have been organized to guide you through a highly engaging consulting project that creates value for your client.

When done correctly these projects can provide an impactful learning experience for everyone involved. Clients receive a thorough consulting report featuring an internal and external analysis along with recommendations tailored to their specific needs. Students receive an opportunity to apply their business knowledge and refine critical thinking and communication skills. The experience can be featured prominently on your resume and used as discussion points in job interviews. This type of professional development can become the factor that separates you from others on the job market.

In closing, it is important to understand the importance of investing your time and energy into this course to gain the full array of benefits. Along the way, be sure to apply yourself in a way that provides value to your team and client. The application component is one of the distinctive elements in these courses. Employers want to hire smart, talented professionals, but ones who understand how to apply their knowledge and create organizational value are the most sought after, particularly if they can effectively articulate what they learned from these projects. This book is designed to guide you along the way and help maximize the benefits gained from this unique experience.

Appendix 1: Templates

Appendix 1A: Survey preamble

We are a group of students in the Team Consulting Program at *insert school* conducting a survey for the benefit of *insert client's name*. If you have any questions about the survey, please contact the team leader, *insert team leader's name*, at *insert team leader's phone and/or email address*. If you have any questions about the Team Consulting Program, please contact the Director, *insert name* at insert phone number or insert email.

[THIS IS RECOMMENDED LANGUAGE FOR THE COVER SHEET THAT A STUDENT TEAM SHOULD USE IF THEY PLAN TO CONDUCT PRIMARY RESEARCH THROUGH THE USE OF A SURVEY]

Appendix 1B: Confidentiality/Participation agreement

Confidentiality and Participation Agreement

In consideration of my being selected for and being permitted to participate in a project that provides advice and assistance to small businesses/organizations, and thus receiving the increased educational experience that will result from my participation, I agree to the following:

1. I agree that I will treat in strict and absolute confidence all information received by me under this project. The only exception of this commitment will be other members of the Project Team, the mentor, and—————————, who will supervise the project.
2. I agree that I will not recommend to the client any purchase of goods or services from sources in which I or other members of the Project Team may have an interest, nor will I accept fees, commissions, gratuities, or other benefits from any firm or individuals that I may recommend to the client.
3. I certify that I am not now involved in a business that competes with my client and will not be involved in such a business during and immediately following the consultation. I hereby agree that I have no rights to compensation for any client improvements resulting from the work in this project.
4. I will maintain confidentiality of any client information permanently. I will never use or discuss any client information except with the Project Team, professor, and mentor during the consulting engagement.
5. I certify that neither myself nor any immediate family member has any interest in the ownership of the client's business.

______________________	______________________
Date	Consultant
______________________	______________________
Date	Consultant
______________________	______________________
Date	Consultant
______________________	______________________
Date	Consultant

Cook, Harris, and Barber III

Appendix 1C: Company contact sheet

COMPANY: ______________ SECTION: ______________

COMPANY CONTACT(S):

NAME	TELEPHONE #	FAX NUMBER	E-MAIL

FACULTY ADVISOR: ______________

TEAM MEMBERS:

NAME	CELL#	OTHER #	E-MAIL ADDRESS	PRIMARY CONTACT PERSON

Appendix 1D: Activity log

Please log the total hours dedicated to the report. Round to the nearest quarter hour and use the following numbering system:

15 minutes = .25 30 minutes = .50 45 minutes = .75 1 hour = 1.00

Week	Discussion and Planning	Meeting with Client	Contact with Client (Phone/ Email)	Research	Writing and Editing	Travel	Presentation	Other	Total
1									
2									
3									
4									
5									
6									
7									
8									
9									
10									
11									
12									
13									
14									
15									

Appendix 1E: List of action verbs

Ironize	Expand	Assume	Justify	Review
Conjecture	Perceive	Denounce	Account	Announce
Illuminate	Manipulate	Renounce	Address	Nod (toward/at)
Expose	Configure	Link	Problematize	Diagnose
Render	Isolate	Gesture (to/at)	Position	Detect
Interpret	Respond	Censure	Inform	Guide
Contradict	Characterize	Contend	Maintain	Persuade
Challenge	Probe	Descend	Conceal	Pronounce
Conflict	Question	Reinforce	Instigate	Coach
Analyze	Evaluate	Bolster	Expound (on)	Adapt
Examine	Highlight	Detach	Recall	Clarify
Study	Emphasize	Broaden	Echo	Craft
Signal	Underscore	Distinguish	Dismiss	Attain
Investigate	Focus	Amplify	Alter	Discuss
Scrutinize	Feature	Intensify	Elevate	Posit
Confirm	Accentuate	Reconfigure	Conflate	Obscure
Verify	Attest	Deride	Negate	Disguise
Create	Initiate	Shroud	Disclose	Trigger
Generate	Shape	Authorize	Enforce	Rationalize
Fashion	Transform	Dramatize	Conceive	Treat
Form	Frame	Illustrate	Augment	Carry
Construct	Support	Present	Identify	Validate
Deconstruct	Sustain	Represent	Witness	Engage
Reconstruct	Suggest	Explain	Attribute	Elaborate (on)
Build	Propose	Prove	Arrange	Condense
Produce	Imply	Demonstrate	Evoke	Connect
Invent	Insinuate	Exhibit	Advance	Defy
Condemn	Indicate	Express	Dismantle	Divulge
Claim	Signify	Reveal	Argue	Warp
Hint	Denote	Establish	Enable	Misconceive
Obstruct	Connote	Offer	Explore	Grasp
Veil	Critique	Exist	Negotiate	Recognize
Dispute	Interrogate	Portray	Mediate	Ascribe
Criticize	Situate	Describe	Simulate	Assign
Consider	Assert	Exemplify	Organize	Radicalize
Access	Complicate	Epitomize	Work (to)	Navigate
Heighten	Associate	Embody	Prioritize	Counteract
Chronicle	Insist	Explicate	Prompt	Traverse
Historicize	Elucidate	Instruct	Contextualize	Lampoon

Appendix 1F: Progress report

(submit 1 per team electronically)

Team name—————— Date: ——————

CLIENT INTERVIEW(S):

Name of firm —————— Person interviewed ——————

Type of interview: at firm —————— telephone ——————
other ——————

Group members present/involved: ——————

Purpose of interview (goals):

Information obtained:

TEAM ACTIVITY (not the interview):

1. Describe any work done this week(s) related to the project:
2. Indicate the sources used in any research that was done:
3. Describe any problem areas you have encountered associated with the project. Have they been successfully overcome?

INDIVIDUAL ACTIVITY (each team member should list his/her name and what they did during this reporting period involving their consulting project):

1. ——————

2. ——————

3. ——————

4. ——————

Appendix 1G: Peer evaluation

This is an anonymous evaluation. Be open, fair, and constructive as you rate each team member **and yourself**. Use a 10-point rating scale, with 10 = superior and 1 = very weak.

Place names in column headings, and totals at bottom of each column.

If you'd like to add any comments, you may do so on the bottom of this form or attach a separate page.

When completed, please email it to —————— or drop it off at ——————. This is due by —————— and counts toward your participation score. Thank you.

Names	Self			
On time/prepared for all group meetings				
Helped keep the group cohesive				
Contributed a number of useful ideas				
Quantity of work done				
Quality of work done				
Totals				

Appendix 2: Examples

Appendix 2A: SWOT example

Internal strengths	**Internal weaknesses**
• New executive director • Access to survey data from businesses and consumers • Recent increase in membership (20 members) • Increase in financial resources ($7,000–$21,000) with new director	• Not enough social media presence • Lack of knowledge given to people on what the Chamber of Commerce provides • Lack of info or assistance with advertising, building improvements, internet, customer service, market analysis • Not enough new programs to fit new interests
External opportunities	**External threats**
• Increased demand for more information meetings (presentations about new events) • Increased demand for interactive dinners/lunch with other companies • Increased demand for new programs created to fit new interests • Increased demand for more access to information or assistance with (for employees): Advertising/Marketing, Building improvements, internet, customer service, market analysis	• Declining population growth • Ageing population • Low median household income • Lack of succession planning for businesses • Low interaction between other businesses

Appendix 2B: TOWS example

1. **Maxi-Maxi Strategy (strategies that use strengths to maximize opportunities)**
   With a new executive director leading the Martin County Chamber of Commerce, the Chamber was able to gain 20 members and nearly triple their bank account. With an increase in financial resources and new access to business and consumer data, the chamber will have the opportunity to satisfy some of the recent demands the county is looking to fulfill. Based on the recent survey information, Martin County should use their improved financial resources and newly inspired leadership to develop programs and events that satisfy the demand for informational meetings, interactive dinners between businesses, new programs to fit new interests, and more access to assistance on advertising, building improvements, internet, customer service, and market analysis.
2. **Maxi-Mini Strategy (strategies that use strengths to minimize threats)**
   In order to mitigate some of the external factors that threaten Martin County, the Chamber of Commerce can utilize their increase in chamber membership to provide more assistance toward improving the interaction of other businesses. In addition, their newly acquired survey data can help allow the Chamber to pinpoint a solution to these external threats.
3. **Mini-Maxi Strategy (strategies that minimize weaknesses by taking advantage of opportunities)**
   With opportunities to satisfy the demand for informational meetings, interactive dinners between businesses, new programs to fit new interests, and more access to assistance on advertising, building improvements, internet, customer service, and market analysis. By satisfying these demands, Martin County will be able to mitigate their weakness of having a lack of information or assistance provided to businesses.
4. **Mini-Mini Strategy (strategies that minimize weaknesses and avoid threats)**
   In order to combat some of the weaknesses and threats that impact the Martin County Chamber of Commerce, the Chamber can indirectly reduce the current threats by creating an attractive environment for businesses to interact in. By resolving some of the current weaknesses in the Chamber, local businesses will have the skills they need to operate effectively. In addition, if more businesses engage and interact with each other, the opportunity for improved business relations and advancement can be achieved. Threats are indirectly mitigated by creating a more attractive and engaging location for new businesses. As a result, more people will choose to stay and do business in Martin County, with the potential for an increase in higher-paying jobs.

Appendix 2C: Sample progress report

TEAM PROGRESS REPORT

Team name: XXX   Date:

INTERVIEWS: Not Applicable

Name of firm______________________   Person interviewed________

Type of interview: at firm___ telephone___ other __________________

Group members present/involved: ____

1) Purpose of interview (goals):

2) Information obtained:

TEAM ACTIVITY (not the interview)**:**
1) Describe any work done this week(s) related to the project:

- Discussed the information to include in the LOE and content of the paper with Dr. Cook
- Continued research on past social media platforms used by firm and best practices
- Started drafting the current social media presence portion

2) Indicate the sources used in any research that was done:

The team used various Internet sources including the Rider University library database to determine best practices for using social media platforms. The team also contacted client to find out more information about previously mentioned platforms and additional platforms the firm is currently on.

3) Describe any problem areas you have encountered associated with the project. Have they been successfully overcome?

The team has not recently encountered any problems related to the project.

Figure App 2C.1 Sample progress report.

INDIVIDUAL ACTIVITY :

1) <u>Student 1</u>
   - Communicated with team members to determine key platforms and begin best practices
   - Began drafting a portion of the 'Best Practices' section
   - Initiated and facilitated group conference call

2) <u>Student 2</u>
   - Communicated with team members to determine key platforms and begin best practices
   - Began drafting a portion of the 'Best Practices' section
   - Corrected the LOE and Table of Contents

3) Student 3
   - Contacted client for information about social media platforms
   - Provided updated information to our mentor
   - Communicated with team members to determine key social media platforms
   - Began drafting a portion of the 'Best Practices' section

Figure App 2C.1 Continued

Appendix 2D: Thank you letter

Date
Client Name
Business
Name Address
City, State Zip

Dear (Client's Name):

It has been a pleasure to work with you in an analysis of your organization. Your cooperation, patience, and enthusiasm made our job much easier and contributed to our learning. We feel you have given us a great opportunity to use our formal education in a real-world application.

Our report makes recommendations based upon your input and our analysis. We hope that the implementation of these recommendations will benefit you.

This report should not be interpreted as the official position of the (school) or its staff. Instead, the report contains the views and opinions of the student team based upon our discussions, observations, investigations, and analysis of both internal and external business conditions relative to your operations.

Any questions or comments you may have should be directed to the student team leader (before graduation on *[date and phone number]*) or to our instructor, (_). Again, thank you.

Sincerely,

Student Team Member Student Team Member

Student Team Member Student Team Member

Appendix 2E: Sample letter of engagement

Student Consulting Team
Rider University

February 29, 2020
Mr. Daniel Josephs
Spruce Industries, Inc.
759 E. Lincoln Avenue
Rahway, NJ 07065

Subject: Letter of Engagement between Spruce Industries, Inc. and Student Consulting Team

The Student Consulting Team is delighted to have the opportunity to work with Spruce Industries. This Letter of Engagement describes the services to be performed and the relevant terms and conditions governing the relationship between Spruce and the Student Consulting Team.

I. Background

Spruce Industries is a small, family-owned business that was bought in 1989 by Hank Josephs. Spruce Industries is a wholesale distributor of janitorial and sanitary products, equipment, and supplies for personal service establishments. Spruce provides the highest level of solutions, support, and sustainability for all of your janitorial supply products, cleaning supplies, tools, and equipment needs. They are known as environmental solutions distributors in the New Jersey and New York area. Spruce specializes in high-quality janitorial and sanitation products for clients that range from colleges and universities to hospitals. (Spruce Ind., n.d.)

Spruce is comprised of 20 employees. Hank Josephs, President of Spruce, is accompanied by his son, Daniel Josephs, and 18 other workers. Daniel Josephs is currently Spruce's Executive Vice President and COO, and he has helped us gain more insight on the needs and problems Spruce Industries encounters.

Over this past year, Daniel Josephs has noticed that their company has increased sales due to an excellent sales team. He would like to better utilize his sales team to expedite their profit margins and clientele.

II. Project objectives

Spruce Industries produces and distributes janitorial and sanitary products to commercial businesses such as schools, religious centers, and physical centers. The industry of janitorial and sanitary products is a fairly competitive industry, and Spruce has some very successful competitors. Because Spruce is a smaller company, they have to learn how to utilize their competitive advantages to better compete in this industry.

Spruce Industries would like the Student Consulting Team of Rider University to uncover a better way to target new customers using market-mapping materials. The company is interested in internal and external analysis on their market spectrum. Spruce Industries has recognized that marketing is a tool in which they can gain more clients in areas that are more profitable to them.

The Student Consulting Team of Rider University looks to conduct research to answer these questions: How can Spruce Industries get a better picture of market segment size and opportunity? What is the real dollar amount available in specific segments? For example, how much money does the religious segment spend on custodial supplies in a given region in New Jersey? Where are Spruce Industries opportunities to grow?

III. Approach

1. In order to meet the objectives of this project, the Student Consulting Team will examine Spruce Industries' current customers, specifically those in the education sector (and even more specifically, public high schools in New Jersey). In addition, the Student Consulting Team will converse with Spruce Industries' sales department to determine what they believed made those customers choose to do business with Spruce and how they determine which schools they plan to target in the future.
2. The Student Consulting Team will conduct secondary research using both scholarly sources and public information to determine which schools would be most optimal for Spruce to target using a combination of data such as number of students, building size, economic standing via zip codes, and distance from Spruce's headquarters.
3. After gathering all of this information, the Student Consulting Team will be able to determine which schools have the potential to be the most profitable for Spruce's sales team to target and in turn present that data

to the sales team. In addition, these data will also allow the Student Consulting Team to determine whether Spruce's idea of potentially charging schools a set dollar amount per student is truly viable or not.

4. After determining the viability of all of the schools that fall into the predetermined subset, New Jersey public high schools, the Student Consulting Team will create a color-coordinated visual map that shall help Spruce Industries' sales team to determine which schools would be the most optimal for them to target.

IV. Client deliverables

1. The Student Consulting Team will formally submit the project data to Spruce Industries in presentation form on or before May 4, 2020 (or a mutually acceptable date) at Rider University.
2. At the time of the presentation, Spruce Industries will receive a bounded copy of the project report containing secondary data and the final recommendations of the Student Consulting Team.
3. The Student Consulting Team will provide Spruce Industries with a "Market Mapping Analysis" outlining guidelines and recommendations for optimizing customer acquisition processes.
4. The Student Consulting Team will look into "by product pricing method" to test the viability of this pricing method to customers, with time permitting.

V. Scope of consulting project/responsibilities

General guidelines

- Objectives and assumptions contained in the project proposal are based on information provided by Mr. Dan Josephs of Spruce Industries to the Student Consulting Team.
- The Letter of Engagement will define the scope of the consulting project.
- Any modifications to project requirements must be agreed to by Mr. Dan Josephs, the Student Consulting Team, and the professor. These modifications must be documented via e-mail or written agreement.

Spruce Industries responsibilities

- Commit the time and resources necessary to provide all requested information, feedback, and guidance on a timely basis.

- Be available to the Student Consulting Team at mutually agreeable times and locations, either via telephone or in person.
- Provide data as needed to complete internal analysis. Key information that is known at this point is listed below:
  - Customer list of Spruce Industries' current customers in the education industry.
  - Contact information with sales representatives of Spruce Industries.
  - Cost per student for high school customers.
  - Data on current high school customers including:
- One report of the following information for the year 2019:
  - Sales to high school customers of Spruce Industries.
  - Current student count of high school customers.
  - Zip code/current township the high school is in.
- Second report with:
  - Three-year sales for high school customers.
  - Three-year students count for those high school customers.

Student consulting team's responsibilities

- Actively participate in all meetings to understand Spruce Industries' requirements and deliverables.
- Remain in regular contact with Mr. Dan Josephs throughout the project. For simplicity, the majority of communication will be through XXX representing the Student Consulting Team as a primary point of contact for Spruce Industries.
- Communicate project requirements openly and precisely.
- Manage project deliverables and timelines.
- Conduct all meetings and exchanges in a professional and courteous manner.
- Maintain the confidentiality of project information.

VI. Project budget

At this stage in the process, no expenses are expected. Should expenses arise during the course of this project, the Student Consulting Team will require prior authorization by Mr. Dan Josephs. Authorization may be in the form of e-mail.

VII. Project schedule

- Initial meeting at Spruce Industries Rahway, New Jersey, office with Mr. Dan Josephs to obtain information about the organization's needs was held on February 7, 2020.
- Letter of Engagement will be completed by February 29, 2020 and sent to Mr. Dan Josephs for his signature.
- Research will be conducted and finalized by the end of April 2020.
- Final recommendations will be presented via PowerPoint and written report to Mr. Dan Josephs by May 4, 2020 (or a mutually acceptable date).

VIII. Agreement

This analysis, recommendation, and final report that will be provided should not be interpreted as the official position of Rider University or its staff. Rather, it will contain the views and opinions of the Small Business Institute's Student Consulting Team based on discussions, observations, investigations, and analysis of Spruce Industries' operations and its business environment.

If circumstances arise that are beyond the control of the Student Consulting Team or Spruce Industries, and the completion of this project cannot be achieved, the Student Consulting Team and Spruce Industries shall jointly take a course of action that is mutually agreeable.

IX. Approval signatures (on file)

Appendix 2F: Final sample project 1 (tied to Appendix 2E)

Spruce Industry's Market Mapping Student Consulting Project

Student A
Student B
Student C
Rider University
PMBA 8384
Dr. Ron Cook
May 11, 2020

Spruce Report – table of contents

I. Executive summary

Spruce Industries is a small, family-owned wholesale distributor of janitorial and sanitary products, equipment, and supplies for public service entities such as schools, recreational centers, and religious centers. Being that Spruce is a small business, they have a smaller platform to advertise their services compared to Home Depot, Imperial Dade, and Atra, their bigger competitors, which results in less opportunity to attract as many clients. Therefore, they have to use business-to-business (B2B) and face-to-face sales to complete the majority of their transactions, which requires defining a strategy of whom to target and gauging if that target attainment is worth the cost of acquisition. Currently, Spruce has been successful in their sales methods of acquiring business. They have grown marginally year by year, with 2019 being their most profitable year. However, Spruce was interested in improving its marketing approach and reached out to Rider's Small Business Institute for improvement suggestions. Rider's Student Consulting Team's analyzed Spruce's situation and developed a market mapping to improve Spruce's sales results, with an emphasis on public school districts.

Within a 30-mile radius of Spruce's location, the Student Consulting Team identified secondary, vocational, and special schools that Spruce is most likely to have success with selling them cleaning products. From public data, the Team created an external analysis to uncover the most potential profitable new clientele for Spruce, based on metrics that broke down each district within that 30-mile radius by average school budget, household income, average per-student budget per school, and number of students/teachers per school. The Team also developed an internal analysis to provide an in-depth understanding of Spruce Industries' sales process compared to best practices as well as analyzed information on Spruce Industries current customers.

Based on the research results, the Team created a market map that compiles the data from all the schools in that 30-mile radius around Spruce. The market map allows Spruce to filter any area of importance they would like to concentrate on to obtain more customers. For example, the map can highlight the highest and lowest student population, highest and lowest average school budget, and so on, in order to maximize potential profit.

The market mapping plan allows Spruce to gain an influx of new customers that fit within the company's goals, through a better focus. However, for Spruce to properly implement the Student Consulting Team's results, they will need to adhere to the strategy provided. Because Spruce is a small company and has limited resources, this plan was designed to be simple and easy to apply. The Team suggests that Spruce begin implementation with immediately updating and uploading their customer list into the market map to allow a more accurate mapping of current and potential clientele. Within that same time period, Spruce's sales team should take the best practices regarding sales processes to create a standardized Spruce sales process. This should allow Spruce to do a better job of tracking sales progress and improve measuring, forecasting, and managing sales. The last step of implementation is route optimization, and it should be put into fruition approximately one or two months after step 1 and 2 are complete. While route optimization was not in the scope of work for the team, it is suggested here as the next logical step to improve efficiency of servicing the expanded customer base. Spruce will need to research route optimization programs to determine the best fit. With these recommendations, Spruce Industries should be able to expand their company and gain more market share in the industry.

II. Company/Project overview

Background on Spruce Industry

Spruce Industries is a small, family-owned business that was bought in 1989 by Hank Josephs. Spruce Industries is a wholesale distributor of janitorial and sanitary products, equipment, and supplies for personal service establishments. Spruce provides the highest level of solutions, support, and sustainability for all janitorial supply products, cleaning supplies, tools, and equipment needs. They are known as environmental solutions distributors in the New Jersey and New York City area. Spruce specializes in high-quality janitorial and sanitation products for clients that range from colleges and universities to hospitals (Spruce Ind., n.d.).

As a company, their purpose is to provide a pathway to a cleaner, healthier, and safer environment for learning, working, and gathering. Their vision is to build a true business partnership, through mutual benefits, shared outcomes, and transparency. Their mission is to collaborate with their customers in identifying, managing, and providing solutions that best fit their environment by being effective, efficient, and responsible (Spruce Ind., n.d.).

Spruce has 20 employees. Hank Josephs, President of Spruce, is accompanied by his son, Daniel Josephs, and 18 other workers. Daniel Josephs is currently Spruce's Executive Vice President and COO and is the main contact for insight on the needs and problems Spruce Industries encounters.

Project overview

During the 2020 spring semester, the Student Consulting Team did a thorough evaluation of Spruce Industries clientele and their market potential for expansion. The Team included breakdowns of each school within a 30-mile radius of Spruce, assessing Spruce's current and potential customer base and their formal sales process/procedures, and determined the allocation of schools' budgets toward cleaning supplies. The result was a market map that should allow Spruce to find potential clientele much easier. Spruce Industries currently has less than 2 percent of secondary education market share in New Jersey. Utilizing the results from the Team, Spruce should be able to expand their reach in this industry sector and make improvements within their company to better keep track of their expansion progress.

III. Industry overview

Spruce Industries is in the janitorial equipment supply wholesaling industry. According to the U.S. Industry NAICS Report, operators sell specialized equipment and supplies used by service establishments (except supplies used in offices, stores, hotels, restaurants, schools, and health, medical, and photographic facilities). Janitorial supplies include carpet- and floor-cleaning equipment, carpet sweepers, vacuuming systems, floor-sanding equipment, and mop wringers (Le, 2020).

As you can see from the chart, the largest percentage of revenue for the janitorial wholesaling industry is made up of janitorial equipment/supplies and beauty and barber equipment/supplies. These are the main forms of income for companies in this industry, making up nearly 50 percent of all revenues. The additional services such as fire alarm replacements and laundry services do benefit the business in small percentages. Most businesses

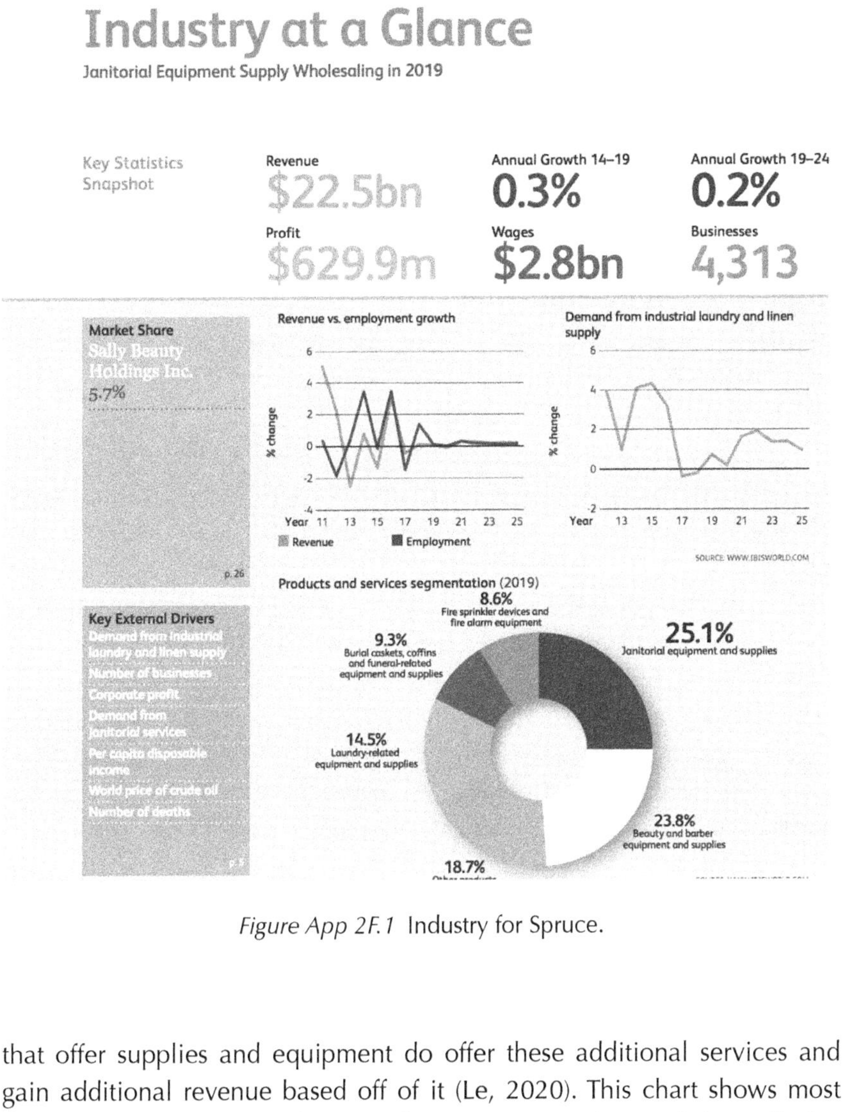

Industry at a Glance

Janitorial Equipment Supply Wholesaling in 2019

Key Statistics Snapshot

Revenue	Annual Growth 14–19	Annual Growth 19–24
$22.5bn	0.3%	0.2%
Profit	**Wages**	**Businesses**
$629.9m	$2.8bn	4,313

Market Share
Sally Beauty Holdings Inc. 5.7%
p. 26

Revenue vs. employment growth
% change
Year 11 13 15 17 19 21 23 25
Revenue Employment

Demand from industrial laundry and linen supply
% change
Year 13 15 17 19 21 23 25
SOURCE: WWW.IBISWORLD.COM

Key External Drivers
Demand from industrial laundry and linen supply
Number of businesses
Corporate profit
Demand from janitorial services
Per capita disposable income
World price of crude oil
Number of deaths
p. 5

Products and services segmentation (2019)
8.6% Fire sprinkler devices and fire alarm equipment
25.1% Janitorial equipment and supplies
9.3% Burial caskets, coffins and funeral-related equipment and supplies
14.5% Laundry-related equipment and supplies
23.8% Beauty and barber equipment and supplies
18.7%

Figure App 2F.1 Industry for Spruce.

that offer supplies and equipment do offer these additional services and gain additional revenue based off of it (Le, 2020). This chart shows most companies focus on supplying to the organization first and then offering other services to help their customers and gain additional revenue off those customers.

The industry profit margins and corporate levels have been declining, which lessens the demand for janitorial equipment and supplies. Because corporate profit margins are in decline, companies are less inclined to spend their discretionary income on janitorial services, equipment, supplies, and products. Fortunately for operators in this industry, not all is bad. There has been a positive offset to corporate decline, which is ageing population growth. IBISWorld forecasts industry revenue will grow at an annualized rate of 0.2 percent to $22.7 billion in the five years to 2024 (Le, 2020). The demand for health and senior services is expected to grow as the boomer generation approaches retirement and declining health. Higher hospital visit rates and lower vacancy rates in eldercare institutions will bolster demand for laundry and linen supply services and janitorial services, benefiting industry operators (Le, 2020).

Business operators in the janitorial equipment supply wholesaling in the United States have both domestic and international competition, which makes competition in the industry medium and increasing. Businesses must first compete with other industry players for customers, but now they have the problem of competing with other industries. Over the past decade, the janitorial equipment supply wholesaling industry has experienced unification of the industry as clients move to purchase products directly from the manufacturer, which makes it harder for new entrants to gain security. They are often unable to get inventory at the same rate as its established competitors (Le, 2020).

Established industry operators are also experiencing a rise in competition from manufacturers and e-commerce sales. Manufacturers allow for clients to skip the middleman and purchase right from them at lower, more reasonable, prices for the same quality item while e-commerce allows for cheaper pricing as well by forgoing the cost of operating inventory in a warehouse (Le, 2020).

Porter's five forces

Threat of new entrants

In the janitorial equipment supply wholesaling industry, there are not any major barriers to enter this business when it comes to initial start-up. If you have a warehouse to distribute out of, or enough capital to purchase a warehouse, you can start to sell. The main barrier comes with gaining customers. The market is mainly dominated by large players in the market that have strong supply chains and economies of scale. These suppliers can supply at a reduced price, which makes it difficult to compete on price. The main way small players compete is by diversifying their services. Another important aspect when looking at the ability for new players to enter is how often the consumers in this market change. The industry runs on a bid process, which means most consumers can change whenever they please. Most stay with the same supplier over long periods, based on price or other factors. It can be difficult for a new supplier to make these consumers change when first starting out. Lastly, when small businesses sell their own brand products it can be difficult to compete against large national distributors, and this can make it more difficult to gain new business. When a consumer is using a large brand that has a strong reputation they are less likely to change to a smaller brand they never heard of. Taking these factors into account the janitorial equipment supply wholesaling industry has a medium threat of new entry, in that it is easy to enter but hard to stay (D, Josephs, personal communication, February 7, 2020).

Rivalry among existing competitors

Distribution

United States/global

i. Home Depot is recently known for selling hardware and doing-it-yourself projects, but it also supplies cleaning products. They have massive distribution centers that can easily handle much larger capacities than any regional player. They also have strong brand recognition and highly competitive pricing due to their size. Home Depot typically sells products directly to consumers but does do B2B business as well. They may not supply small buyers such as a local school, but these businesses can buy from them directly without a formal process (Home Depot, 2020).
ii. Imperial is a janitorial supply distributor located in Jersey City and has been growing quickly. It is close to $2 billion in sales and backed by Bain Capital. Recently, to expand, they have been buying up small companies to expand their operations to a wider market and to have additional capacity. They are located all around the United States, but mostly in Texas, California, Florida, and New Jersey. The only way to purchase from them is to register on their site and buy in bulk, as you cannot go and buy single products (Imperial Dade, 2020). The main threat to Spruce is attempts by Imperial to acquire Spruce and by gaining market share in New Jersey, which makes it more difficult for Spruce to gain new customers.

Regional

i. Atra is another regional player in the New Jersey area, located in Pompton Plains, New Jersey. They are similar in size to Spruce and sell within the same market and are within 30-mile radius from Spruce Industry. Their main consumers are schools, and this means they compete with Spruce for the same customers. They do have a Goes Green program but are not as prevalent as Spruce's sustainability program. Atra also has repair services similar to Spruce's repair services. This is the main regional player Spruce competes against regularly for customers (Atra Janitorial Supply Co., 2020).
ii. North East Janitorial is located in Pompton Lakes, New Jersey and is also in a very close proximity to both Atra and Spruce. All three of these companies are competing in the same industry in the same region. Customers can more freely pick products on their site compared to Spruce and Atra (NorthEast Janitorial Supply Co., 2020).

Service

Cintas is a large corporation that specializes in facility services and can potentially work into the janitorial supplies area. Facility services include supplying disinfectants, mats, restroom supplies, and cleaning services. It would be very easy for them to begin to sell more janitorial products to their existing customers and acquire new customers due to their strong brand name. Cintas also provides similar services to Spruce, specifically looking at their first aid replacement service and cleaning services. They currently are not a huge threat to Spruce, but as Spruce expands and Cintas moves into new markets it can become competition in the future in both services and distribution (Cintas, 2020).

Threat of substitutes

Janitorial supplies are a commodity that anyone can sell. The price for one product is fairly similar across all distributors. This makes it easy for a consumer to find the same product from a different distributor at the same or lower prices, making the threat of substitutes high (Le, 2020).

Bargaining power of suppliers

Distributors have multiple suppliers that can give them a wide range of deals. The most common deal that a distributor can get is for buying in bulk. Usually, there are set price ranges depending on how much they buy, and they get a bigger discount by buying more. There are only a few long-time sellers that will give special offers based on how long the distributor has worked with them. The distributor itself does not have the power to negotiate the deal itself since most of the products are generic and the prices are standardized, but they can switch to a different supplier if needed. The suppliers themselves have no real power on the distributor. Therefore, the suppliers have very little bargaining power (Le, 2020).

Bargaining power of buyers

Distributors often operate through a bid process and usually have deals with their customers for a year or less, and some customers can leave at any given time as well. As the consumer does not have any major obligation to stay with a distributor or only use one supplier, the bargaining power of buyers is high (D, Josephs, personal communication, February 7, 2020).

SWOT analysis of Spruce

Strengths

i. Sustainability/environmentally friendly angle
ii. Capability to establish long-lasting relationships with clients
iii. Flexibility/customization available regarding services offered to clients
iv. Face-to-face contact with clients on behalf of the sales team helps to establish relationships

Spruce, despite being a smaller, local company, has a number of strengths that it can use to its advantage. Spruce is a company that offers a variety of sustainable products, which is unusual for this industry. While they also give clients the option to purchase less-sustainable alternatives, the fact that they offer these products, to begin with, sets them apart from their competition. In addition, Spruce's sales team utilizes face-to-face sales tactics, allowing them to build warmer relationships with potential clients that have the capability to grow to be long-lasting (some clients have worked with Spruce for

25+ years). Spruce also offers a variety of services to its clients that help to differentiate them from their competitors. These include machine repair services, first-aid kit restocks, and even laundry service. This flexibility and customization of services allow Spruce to meet the exact needs of their clients and helps to set them apart from other companies in their industry, thus making it one of Spruce's greatest strengths.

Weaknesses

i. Lack of brand recognizability and subpar online presence
ii. Can't compete on price with larger-scale competitors such as Home Depot
iii. Education sales are not as far-reaching as they ideally would be – 45 percent of business comes from the education sector, but the company only has 2 percent of the market share
iv. Unorganized sales data make conducting analytics research on the company difficult

One of Spruce's biggest weaknesses comes in the form of their online presence. Their social media presence has not been updated, and much of their website is still unfinished. This makes it difficult for potential clients to do any research on the company before contacting them, decreasing the likelihood that they will opt to work with Spruce. In addition, because some of their major competitors are large, international businesses such as Home Depot, it is nearly impossible for Spruce to compete on price, making the services they offer even more valuable. Furthermore, Spruce's sales operations in the education sector are not operating to their full potential. Despite 45 percent of their business coming from the education sector, they only possess 2 percent of the market share in New Jersey. While managing to maintain long-lasting connections with many of their clients in this sector, they have not been able to gain new customers in all of the schools surrounding their customer base. Another weakness that Spruce has comes in the form of its data organization. Rather than having the sales data for their products itemized, they are simply categorized, meaning that the company can tell you how many units of hand soap that they sold in a given period, but not which specific brands of hand soap were the bestsellers. This makes drawing conclusions regarding these analytics extremely difficult.

Opportunities

i. Revamping of the company website/social media presence
ii. Increased push to gain market share with recreational centers (i.e. YMCA's)
iii. Determining which school zones have the most profit potential for optimized targeting
iv. Highlighting the unique services offered by Spruce that differentiate them from their competitors

Spruce has many opportunities that they can take advantage of in order to leverage themselves into a more optimal position. For example, if they were to update their website and social media, potential clients will be able to get a better understanding of the company prior to contacting them and maybe more inclined to do business with them. Spruce has also recently made a push to enter recreational centers and has begun supplying several YMCAs in New Jersey. If they can leverage these relationships that they've established, they may be able to gain more YMCAs and increase their market share in this sector. A large portion of Spruce's business comes from the education sector. By determining which schools have the greatest profitability by seeing how much they spend on janitorial supplies per student, Spruce can push to more effectively target these high-profit schools. Finally, by promoting their unique service-based offerings to customers, Spruce can help themselves to stand out to potential clients.

Threats

i. Low-cost large providers and online retailers undercutting Spruce's business
ii. Any downturn in the economy leads people to care less about what is sustainable and more about the brands that they know they can get for a cheap price
iii. Customers decide to stick with cleaning products that they are familiar with and refuse to make the switch to Spruce's in-house brand
iv. Companies such as Cintas beginning to encroach on Spruce's market share

One of Spruce's major threats comes in the form of its competitors. Large competitors such as Home Depot can undercut them on price, and e-commerce sites such as Amazon can be seen as more convenient, making it extremely difficult for a company the size of Spruce to compete. In addition, in an economic downturn, people may be less inclined to care about services or sustainability and more likely to opt for lower-priced alternatives. On top of this, Spruce as a brand lacks the brand recognizability that may exist with its competitors, which could make customers more likely to stick with companies that they recognize, especially with the lack of information about Spruce that is available online. Spruce uses a business model that is similar to the company Cintas in regard to their services. However, as they begin to become more like Cintas, the inverse is also true, and Cintas can become more like Spruce; this means that Cintas could become an additional competitor that Spruce has to battle.

IV. External customer analysis

Background

Spruce Industries is located in Rahway, New Jersey. This location presents Spruce with plenty of business opportunities that Spruce's sales associates can contact to start a new relationship. Within a 30-mile radius of Spruce, there are 1,470 different secondary, vocational, and special schools. Within those schools are a diverse range of prospects that the Student Consulting Team will help Spruce decipher. The Team will identify the best options for Spruce Industries to pursue by providing a breakdown analysis of these targets' proximity to Spruce, budget size, area income, and student count, along with the square footage of the school. Spruce Industries would seem to have almost endless potential clients to consider, but because of the company's size and its competition, Spruce should focus on specific schools.

The Team has created a spreadsheet that breaks down each school in this radius by the zip code, district, and county it resides, household income by district, median income by zip code, estimated overall school budget, per-student budget, locale, number of students and teachers, grade, and the overall student and teacher count. In the 30-mile radius around Spruce, there are 12 different New Jersey counties: Bergen, Camden, Essex, Hudson, Hunterdon, Mercer, Middlesex, Monmouth, Morris, Passaic, Somerset, and Union.

Summary statistics

We collected data from the National Center of Education Statistics and the New Jersey Department of Education for each county in the 30-mile radius of Spruce Industries. Some statistics in the specific county may vary due to only part of the county being included. These are for K-12 public school districts. Summary data are as follows:

Bergen County has 227 schools, and of those schools there are 59 districts in which they all reside.

- Household Income by District: $91,572
- Locale: Large Suburban Schools
- Average Median Income by Zip Code: $84,878
- Average Estimated School Budget: $10,865,576
- Average Per-Student Budget Amount: $24,237
- Average Number of Students Per School: 481
- Average Number of Teachers Per School: 40

Camden County has 1 school that resides in 1 district.

- Household Income by District: $65,073
- Average Median Income by Zip Code: $31,137
- Average Estimated School Budget: $25,724,160
- Average Per-Student Budget Amount: $22,968
- Average Number of Students Per School: 1120
- Average Number of Teachers Per School: 57

Essex County has 225 schools, and of those schools there are 44 districts in which they all reside.

- Household Income by District: $57,365
- Average Median Income by Zip Code: $67,118
- Average Estimated School Budget: $13,287,312
- Average Per-Student Budget Amount: $22,599
- Average Number of Students Per School: 592
- Average Number of Teachers Per School: 46

Hudson County has 124 schools, and of those schools there are 25 districts in which they all reside.

- Household Income by District: $62,681
- Average Median Income by Zip Code: $55,795

- Average Estimated School Budget: $15,397,099
- Average Per-Student Budget Amount: $22,146
- Average Number of Students Per School: 702
- Average Number of Teachers Per School: 53

Hunterdon County has 12 schools, and of those schools there are six districts in which they all reside.

- Household Income by District: $110,969
- Average Median Income by Zip Code: $85,549
- Average Estimated School Budget: $7,878,779
- Average Per-Student Budget Amount: $26,950
- Average Number of Students Per School: 297
- Average Number of Teachers Per School: 34

Mercer County has 19 schools, and of those schools there are five districts in which they all reside.

- Household Income by District: $77,027
- Average Median Income by Zip Code: $114,336
- Average Estimated School Budget: $17,005,421
- Average Per-Student Budget Amount: $22,433
- Average Number of Students Per School: 777
- Average Number of Teachers Per School: 63

Middlesex County has 191 schools, and of those schools there are 26 districts in which they all reside.

- Household Income by District: $83,133
- Average Median Income by Zip Code: $80,248
- Average Estimated School Budget: $13,434,790
- Average Per-Student Budget Amount: $19,529
- Average Number of Students Per School: 684
- Average Number of Teachers Per School: 54

Monmouth County has 151 schools, and of those schools there are 43 districts in which they all reside.

- Household Income by District: $91,807
- Average Median Income by Zip Code: $89,646
- Average Estimated School Budget: $12,687,630
- Average Per-Student Budget Amount: $23,496

- Average Number of Students Per School: 549
- Average Number of Teachers Per School: 49

Morris County has 140 schools, and of those schools there are 39 districts in which they all reside.

- Household Income by District: $107,034
- Average Median Income by Zip Code: $105,135
- Average Estimated School Budget: $11,538,444
- Average Per-Student Budget Amount: $22,969
- Average Number of Students Per School: 503
- Average Number of Teachers Per School: 45

Passaic County has 132 schools, and of those schools there are 25 districts in which they all reside.

- Household Income by District: $63,339
- Average Median Income by Zip Code: $52,649
- Average Estimated School Budget: $14,141,914
- Average Per-Student Budget Amount: $24,552
- Average Number of Students Per School: 583
- Average Number of Teachers Per School: 46

Somerset County has 79 schools, and of those schools there are 59 districts in which they all reside.

- Household Income by District: $106,046
- Average Median Income by Zip Code: $100,040
- Average Estimated School Budget: $14,485,450
- Average Per-Student Budget Amount: $21,484
- Average Number of Students Per School: 673
- Average Number of Teachers Per School: 60

Union County has 169 schools, and of those schools there are 59 districts in which they all reside

- Household Income by District: $73,376
- Average Median Income by Zip Code: $78,992
- Average Estimated School Budget: $11,849,184
- Average Per-Student Budget Amount: $20,505
- Average Number of Students Per School: 564
- Average Number of Teachers Per School: 45

Key statistical metrics

Based on the information found, we broke down some key criteria that would make certain schools ideal clients for Spruce. The following criteria are what we believe represent the most potential profitable school districts:

- Household Income by District
- Estimated School Budget
- Number of Students
- Average Per-Student Budget

One of the key statistics that we looked at was the number of students in each district. The number of students can signal that these districts have a higher budget for these schools. We see Essex and Middlesex counties have some of the highest student counts, compared to Mercer and Hunterdon County which have some of the lowest student counts. It is important to note some counties were not captured in full, due to their distance from Spruce. However, we do not want to remove these counties completely based on the

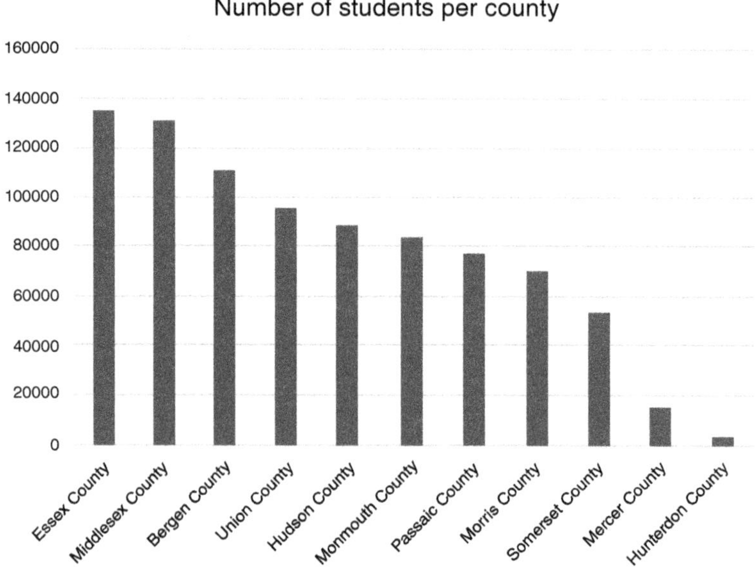

Figure App 2F.2 Students per county.

distance factor alone, but they should not be considered as one of the more profitable targets unless Spruce wants to expand its area of scope. Further analysis of these areas would need to be done to understand their true value.

Looking at specific zip codes in Figure App 2F.3, we can see that specific areas spend more per student than others (note: since New Jersey zip codes begin with a 0, the table from excel shows the last four numbers). The top three that spend the most per student are Paramus (7652 – Bergen County), Asbury Park (7712 – Monmouth County), and Patterson (7502 – Passaic). These three areas are some of the top targets for Spruce to look at when it comes to the largest potential profit, as these would be looked at as high potential profit zip codes. The schools in these areas generally have the highest budgets for the lowest amount of students/schools. One thing to note is that there is a string of Passaic county zip codes that have the exact same cost per student regardless of budget size, equaling $30,527 per student cost. We did not see such a high-standard cost per student in zip codes across any other county.

Figure App 2F.4 shows which schools have the most students, based first on those top cost-per-student areas from Figure App 2F.2. This matters since more students with higher cost per student means the district will have a higher budget. This showed that there is a correlation with the select schools in these zip codes and high student populations. These top three zip codes have the highest cost per student, high median income, and high population of students and would be ideal for Spruce to look into as potential clients.

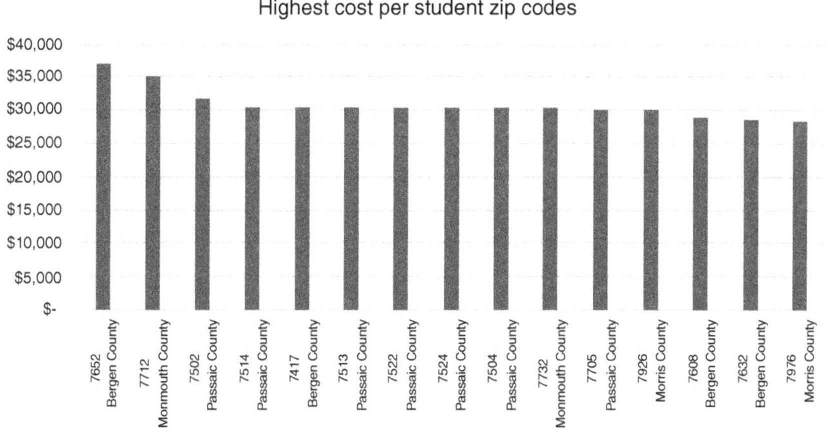

Figure App 2F.3 Spending per zip code.

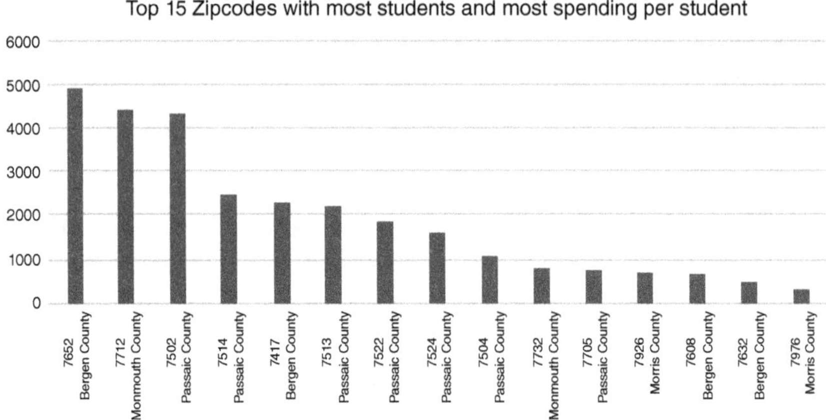

Figure App 2F.4 Students and spending.

The schools in the 7652 – zip code of Bergen County (Paramus), 7712 – zip code of Monmouth County (Asbury Park), and the 7502 – zip code of Passaic County (Paterson) are also notable as being districts with some of the highest profits per student, and they would be optimal for Spruce to target as big potential clients based on schools in that geographic area code.

Analysis of potential clients for Spruce

A quick analysis of the geographical breakdown of the financial statistics of the school and households within a 30-mile radius of Spruce Industries headquarters can lead to some interesting conclusions. For example, Bergen County, Hunterdon County, and Morris County, despite being three of the top five counties in respect to household income by district, have the three lowest average estimated school budgets of any of the counties relevant to this exercise. This means that the financial status of a specific county of New Jersey does not directly translate to the most financially well-off schools. Therefore, if we are to determine which schools might be the most ideal for Spruce Industries to target, we must be looking at the full scope of factors available to us.

The prioritization of different targeting criteria can have a great impact on which school districts within specific counties should be targeted. For example, take Passaic County. Despite only having a household income by district of $63,339, it has an estimated school budget of $14,141,914. In addition, Passaic County has an average per-student budget of $24,552, second only to Hunterdon County which has a lot fewer schools and a significantly higher household income by district. Of the 132 schools within Passaic County, 131 fall into the classification of "large suburban," and thus the average data are very close to the data that you would find for large suburban schools. All of these data would seem to lead to the conclusion that Passaic County would be an ideal location for Spruce to target. However, there is still another factor at play. The schools within Passaic County have an average number of 583 students, which is not small, but is mid-sized compared to the other counties. If Spruce were seeking to target larger schools, as they are more likely to spend higher amounts for janitorial supplies, then finding the largest schools within Passaic County might be a good way for the company to go.

Therefore, looking at the larger schools within Passaic County can allow us to make observations regarding which particular districts might be the most worthwhile for Spruce to target. For example, while the Passaic County School District does have some of the largest schools within the county, its median income by zip code is lower than other areas at $34,291, meaning that the schools in this district are likely not the most well-off financially. Instead, it might make more sense for Spruce to target schools in the Wayne Township Public School District. The median income by zip code of households that are in this district is much higher at $104,063, than both Passaic County School District and even the Passaic County household income by district. In particular, two schools within this district, Wayne Hills High School and Wayne Valley High School, are both financially well-off and both fall into the top ten in regard to number of students, making both of these schools ideal targets for Spruce.

The information regarding targeting Passaic County would be relevant if Spruce were to prioritize targeting schools that are financially well-off. However, if Spruce were to prioritize their targeting efforts specifically toward schools that have larger student populations, then they may have to redirect their efforts toward different areas, such as Hudson County and Mercer County. Mercer County has significantly fewer schools than either Passaic or Hudson. However, with an average estimated school budget of $17,005,421 and the largest average number of students at

777, there are still several schools here that could be ideal clients for Spruce to pursue. Princeton High School, Hightstown High School, and West Windsor-Plainsboro High School South are all financially well-off and have student populations of over 1,600, thus making them excellent potential clients for Spruce Industries. Hudson County, despite not being as strong financially as some of the other relevant counties, does have several schools that have large student populations as well as reasonable budgets. Within Hudson County, the district that may be the most ideal to focus on would likely be Jersey City Public Schools. Four of the top ten schools within Hudson County, budget wise, fall into the Jersey City Public Schools district, and a portion of the schools in this district have over 1,000 students. Of the schools in this district, some of the ones that Spruce may want to focus on would be William L. Dickinson High School and James J. Ferris High School. Both have over 1,300 students and are in the top 10 budget-wise for Hudson County, making them ideal potential clients for Spruce (Table App 2F.1).

Table App 2F.1 Top Counties Utilizing Key Metrics

Highest Household Income	County Name	County Household Income
	Hunterdon County	$110,969
	Morris County	$107,034
	Somerset County	$106,046
Average Per-Student Budget Amount	County Name	County Average Per-Student Budget Amount
	Hunterdon County	$26,950
	Passaic County	$24,552
	Bergen County	$24,237
Average Number of Students Per School[a]	County Name	County Average Student Number Per School
	Mercer County	777
	Hudson County	702
	Middlesex County	684

[a] Camden County not considered as it contains only one school in one district.

V. Internal consumer analysis

The sales process

In a review of Spruce's sales process, Dan Josephs indicated that Spruce begins this process with their sales team prospecting and contacting district boards of education, but they do not have a standardized, formal process for doing this. They then negotiate and try to sell their products to the potential new customer. Once an agreement is reached, a contract is put together between Spruce and the board of education to supply specific products to the schools in those districts (D, Josephs, personal communication, April 9, 2020). We examined this process through the criteria that Spruce uses to find new potential clients and also the process itself.

Internal Spruce Industries analysis

The sales process and Dan Josephs' feedback revealed that Spruce uses student counts and the number of schools in the district versus our external analysis, where we used estimated budgets, student count, and average spending per student as our criteria. The common factor that both analyses used was student count. After learning about the criteria Spruce uses to look at new customers, we used actual sales and a sample customer list from Spruce to complete our analysis. We consolidated the information that we received from Spruce's customers at a district level and the database of schools from our external analysis and looked at all of the information at a district level. We found the districts with the most schools were Newark, Paterson, and Jersey City. Looking at the districts with the most students, we saw Newark, Elizabeth, and Jersey City had the highest student counts in the district. We then looked at Spruce's client list to see what customers they already do business with and which ones they do not sell anything too. Using Spruce's criteria, our list of schools/districts, and Spruce's current customers, we can find which districts Spruce can target as clients. This will be discussed further in our market mapping section.

Limitations to current Spruce data

Lacking sales information on specific products

Spruce sells a wide variety of products to each customer. The customer will negotiate with Spruce on the products it needs and then Spruce will supply these products over the course of the contract. There is not a standardized package of products. Some will be supplied only cleaning chemicals while others would receive toiletries and still others might receive school supplies such as paper. Generally, Spruce does not supply all of their products to each school. This makes sales volume and products to each school different based on what products they get from Spruce. To be able to forecast potential new customers for Spruce, we would need to look at product-level sales from Spruce's information. However, this information was listed by category only (i.e. mops vs. a specific type of mop). Hence, we found that there was not a consistent product-level factor across multiple districts that would help predict sales.

Discrepancies in internal and external data

We were not able to link specific districts by name from Spruce's customer list to our external school database. However, we were able to find a common factor between the internal Spruce customer list and the external report, which was by zip code. It was effective in most cases, but there are some universities and community colleges in the current customer list from Spruce. This would make the link between our report and Spruce's customer list slightly inaccurate when looking at what business Spruce currently does. A complete list of Spruce's customers that are only public K-12 school districts would be a more effective method of linking districts.

Another thing to note is that the external data did not contain all the information needed. While it did include all the schools in districts, some of the schools were missing student counts, which would make the district student counts inaccurate.

Formal sales process

Most salespeople do not follow imposed routines. According to the Objective Management Group, 68 percent of all salespeople do not follow a sales process (Plaksji, 2020). Spruce's sales team is among those who do not have a standard process. We interviewed the top salesperson at Spruce Industries, who sold over 2 million dollars in supplies last year alone. When asked, "What is your full process of approaching and securing a client?" he responded by citing different methods to reach their prospective customers. He has no standardized sales routine, but he is successful in making sales. Research suggested, as noted below, that having a distinct routine can improve sales success.

"A sales process is a set of repeatable steps that a sales person takes to take a prospective buyer from the early stage of awareness to a closed sale. Typically, a sales process consists of 5–7 steps: Prospecting, Preparation, Approach, Presentation, Handling Objections, Closing, and Follow-up" (Plaksji, 2020: sec. 2, para. 2). It is the potential customer's journey of realization that they need Spruce. This is a very basic process that most sales personnel are aware of but many sales people, as noted by the 68 percent figure cited above, decide not to follow it. Most sales people don't bother with standardizing their processes as long as they are closing deals and bringing in revenue, but many can benefit from a standardized sales process and improved measuring, forecasting, and general management of sales (Plaksji, 2020).

According to a research by the Sales Management Association, "90% of all companies that use a formal, guided sales process were ranked as the highest performing" (Plaksji, 2020: sec. 3, para. 3). TAS Group and *Harvard Business Review* have conducted studies that prove that companies who implement a sales process outperform companies that choose not to. TAS Group says, "70% of the companies that follow a structured process in sales are high performers; over 70% of business forecasts were accurate for the companies with a defined sales process" (Plaksji, 2020: sec. 3, para. 5). A study by *Harvard Business Review* showed that "businesses with a standardized sales process see up to a 28% increase in revenue" compared to businesses that do not (Jordan & Kelly, 2015: para 5). *Harvard Business Review* also reveals that "50% of high-performing sales organizations admit having closely monitored, strictly enforced or automated sales processes." Meanwhile, "48% of under-performing organizations have non-existent or informal sales processes" (Martin, 2017: para 7). These studies show that revenue, performance, and forecasting accuracy are influenced significantly when a company or sales person adapts to a standardized sales process.

Therefore, the Spruce's sales team should adopt a standardized process. This process will help each sales team member and associate keep track of the pathway to their end goal. "Knowing what each step entails, helps salespeople to understand where they are in the process, when it's time to move to the next step and when to adjust your course" (Plaksji, 2020: sec. 4, para. 5). Spruce defining their sales processes could result in gaining a more accurate understanding of whether their system to attract and keep clients is functional or nonfunctional. It should help the team identify the right operations and get rid of wasteful activities that yield little to no results.

The standardization of a sales process may be scripted, but it does not have to limit the ability to be creative. The sales process won't be a word-for-word formula to use on each client or dictate how to sell to certain people. Rather, it creates a backbone to the fundamental aspects of the method. By having a regulated system, companies are able to find the cause of stalled sales by analyzing "whether or not your actions were sufficient, how many of them you actually needed, and what proved to be a misstep or a waste of time" (Plaksji, 2020: sec. 4, para. 11).

School budget allocation toward janitorial supplies

Janitorial supplies are but one of the many expenditures that schools have to consider when allocating the funds within their given budgets. Some of the other key expenses that schools must consider when choosing how to break down their budgets include administrative expenses, employee salaries, and instructional expenditures. Each school district within the state of New Jersey is going to have a different budgetary breakdown, meaning that they are going to allocate their resources in a different manner. For example, some districts with smaller schools with fewer students may be able to get away with spending less of their allocated budgets on custodial supplies and may choose to spend the bulk of their money on administrative expenses and student instruction tools. However, districts that contain larger schools with greater student populations may have to put more of their budget toward janitorial supplies in order to accommodate their greater number of students. Due to the great disparity that exists among school sizes within various districts across New Jersey, there is not a great deal of uniformity when it comes to how these different schools have chosen to allocate their given budgets, as different districts have had to make particular decisions in order to accommodate their specific needs. Therefore, the best way to determine what New Jersey schools as a whole allocate toward janitorial supplies would be to look at their average spending.

However, there is not a great deal of information available regarding specifically how much each district in New Jersey spends on their janitorial supplies and custodial needs. The National Center for Education Statistics', or NCES', website has a feature that can allow users to see the fiscal breakdown of a specific school district's spending. For example, we looked at the budgetary breakdown of the Passaic City School District and found that there is no real indication of how janitorial services in particular are incorporated into the budget. It is likely that they would be considered to be a part of the "Operations, Food Service, other" category, but that is not explicitly stated. However, on nj.gov, a taxpayers' guide to education spending can be found. This guide breaks down education spending into different categories and presents the data on a per-student basis. Even here, spending on janitorial supplies is not explicitly stated. However, one of the categories, "Total Operations and Maintenance of Plants," includes the cost of custodial services alongside a number of other costs that schools must stay on top of, including but not limited to heating, lighting, and grounds keeping (New Jersey Department of Education, 2020). According to the website, the Total Operations and Maintenance of Plants spending consisted of $1,985 per pupil (New Jersey Department of Education, 2020). While this is not exclusively the per-pupil amount that is spent on janitorial supplies, it does provide a more in-depth look at how schools are allocating their budgets in regard to custodial services than the NCES' available information.

VI. Market mapping

Market mapping data process

The market map for Spruce industries was created through compiled data of public schools within a 30-mile radius of Spruce. We then compiled the data to a district level and kept all relevant information that would be used in the market mapping. This information included district name, county name, city, state, zip code, estimated district budget, student and teacher count per school, if Spruce does business in that zip code, number of schools per district, and estimated maximum potential sales. Estimated budgets for schools were gathered through district budget information from a database for all school districts in New Jersey. The list of zip codes and districts that Spruce does business with was from a customer list from Spruce, along with sales numbers for each customer. The sales numbers were used to check for a method to predict sales for new potential clients and to find what the maximum potential sales could be for all districts. This calculation was developed using the Edison school as a benchmark. Edison was used because it is a district where Spruce sells all janitorial supplies to Edison public school district (D, Josephs, personal communication, February 7, 2020). The data were then compiled into an excel mapping graph which was broken out into regions of New Jersey by zip code within a 30-mile radius of Spruce's office. The map is highlighted by the highest and lowest student population. Student population was determined to be the common factor across both the internal and external analysis to predict the maximum amount of potential sales. This can be filtered by the district-level spreadsheet to show where Spruce does and does not do business and any other metrics (see the spreadsheet accompanying this report, and samples in Appendix 1).

Market map instructions

The market map contains two maps; one shows if Spruce does business in that area or not, and the second map shows the highest and lowest of the set criteria. The criteria currently are color-coded in Figure App 2F.1 by red, green, and blue (red if Spruce does not do business, green is Spruce does business, and blue is Spruce's location). The same color coding is used for the Figure App 2F.2 map for simplicity but can be altered in the spreadsheet if Spruce wants to overlay them, as this lets Spruce set multiple criteria on one map. The two maps are shown in the market map section (Figures App 2F.5 and App 2F.6) in Appendix 1. These maps are generated from the zip codes in the district-level data spreadsheet, since the district names in Spruce's customer list vary from government websites. Spruce can use the filter option in the district-level spreadsheet to change what criteria and data it shows. For the criteria of if Spruce does business or not within a school, 1 will represent if Spruce does business, 0.5 will represent Spruce, and 0 will be if Spruce does not do business with that school. A visual is shown in Figure App 2F.7 in Appendix 1. Once you adjust the data with the filter options, you can highlight the sections on the map and it will show a zip code and value, and the value will be dependent on what criteria are selected, as shown in Figure App 2F.8 (Appendix 1). You can use the filter section in the zip code column to look at what specific districts make up that zip code. The final step will be to update the customer list with new customers; this is shown in Figure App 2F.9 (Appendix 1). This will be updated with the name of the customer, town, state, and zip code. This will update the spreadsheet column if Spruce does business in that section of any spreadsheet and in the market map.

Approximately every five years, the data in the database should be updated to account for changes in student count and school budget changes. You would use the NCES database. On their website, they have a large database of all types of schools. The filter we used to download the data can be found using this link: https://nces.ed.gov/ccd/districtsearch/district_list.asp?Search=1&State=34&Zip=07065&Miles=30

Once at this link you can click the link to download the excel spreadsheet and copy and paste the same columns in the by school-level spreadsheet.

The NCES also holds information on private schools and colleges that can be used to increase the range and the amount of schools. This can be used to create other market maps of different sectors. If you want to see the other ranges of data, you can go under the menu and under data and tools you can see all the data the NCES has to offer.

Results

In order to make it clear which locations on the map would be the most ideal for Spruce to target, a color gradient scale was implemented. Zip codes that include school districts that have higher student populations, which as mentioned above is the main factor in consideration when choosing potential new clients in the education sector, will have brighter green shading on the map. In turn, zip codes that include school districts that have smaller student populations are going to be indicated by brighter red. Duller green areas represent zip codes with higher student populations, but not areas where this is at the highest, while duller red areas represent zip codes that have lower student populations but are not the lowest overall. This gradient color scale makes it easier to interpret the map. The sales team at Spruce can determine which specific zip codes to focus on using this color gradient to find a high density of high population schools. For example, the Newark Public School District has the highest student count of any of the school districts, with a student count of 35,713. This school district falls into the zip code of 07103. Therefore, because there is a high student density within that zip code, it would appear to be shaded bright green on the map. However, there are also a number of smaller charter schools with fewer students within this same zip code. This is where the rest of the spreadsheet can be useful, as the Spruce sales team will be able to filter for that specific zip code and determine which districts within that high-student-density area are the most ideal to target. Overall, by making use of the color gradient map, in conjunction with the other features and capabilities of the spreadsheet (which contains key information regarding the attractiveness of specific schools as potential targets), Spruce's sales team will be able to make clear and informed targeting decisions within the education sector.

VII. Conclusion and recommendations

The main recommendation that our team has for Spruce's sales team would be to utilize the information available to them via the spreadsheet and market map to make better decisions about which schools they should be targeting. Currently, Spruce uses sales methods such as cold calling and information tips to determine which schools they should try to sell to, rather than having a formal sales process to follow when making such determinations. However, if Spruce's sales team were to utilize the information provided within the spreadsheet and the market map, they would be better able to determine which schools would be optimal for them to target. The market map can provide them with a visual on which specific New Jersey zip codes have the highest student density, which is the most important factor for Spruce to consider as it directly translates to the amount of supplies that a school would need to purchase. By placing their headquarters on this map, Spruce would also be able to determine which zip codes with high student densities that are close to them or that are near their existing customers. This would allow them to optimize the potential routes that their trucks would have to take to deliver these supplies to the schools, making these additional trips a worthwhile investment for the company. Spruce's sales team would also be able to utilize the filters on the spreadsheet to determine which specific districts they should attempt to sell to by doing things such as narrowing the results to include only zip codes with high student population densities or by including other factors, such as school budgets, into their analysis. Overall, it is our hope for Spruce, and specifically their sales team, that the information provided to them within the spreadsheet and the market map leads them to reorganize the process by which they select school districts to target and helps them focus on target schools that would bring in the most revenue.

VIII. Implementation

For Spruce to implement the market map, multiple steps will need to be taken to fully integrate the map. The three steps that they will need to take will be to update customer data, develop and implement a formal sales process, and optimize their sales representatives' routes. Below is an implementation schedule for Spruce to follow over the next few months to implement the market map.

May 2020
• 5/15 – Spruce first needs to import a full current customer list of all public schools and clean the customer list of all schools that do not fit the criteria of K-12 public schools. The customer list will be inserted into the customer list input tab in the following columns: Districts, Town, State, and Zip Code.
By August 2020
• Spruce will need to develop a formal sales process for its sales representatives to ensure that they have the best process of acquiring customers. Spruce can use the recommendations and the information given in the formal sales process section of our report along with conversations with the sales team on best practices to develop a formal sales process that makes sense for Spruce. • TBD – due to the coronavirus, sales may be unpredictable. Spruce should look to start the new formal sales process once the pandemic is over so they can see true results for the formal sales process and study if the new process increases sales and customer acquisition. Hence, the date of the new sales process being integrated into Spruce will be unknown at this point in time.
By end of 2020
• Once the customer list is updated in the market map and the formal sales process is fully developed, Spruce can look into implementing a method of route optimization with the market map. The market map gives a visual of where Spruce is relative to its current customers and possible customers. With a third-party program, Spruce can use the locations of its current customers in the market map and find the closest, most profitable, potential customers. This allows Spruce's sales representatives to visit a current client and a potential client in the same trip. • If Spruce does not already have software, there are multiple programs that can help them with route optimization to ensure Spruce's sales representatives have extra supplies/samples to visit potential customers while on trips to current customers.
January 2021 onward
• Spruce can use the market map in multiple ways, including forecasting potential sales for new customers and sales for current customers based on product sales. Spruce can look to further develop the market map by adding more information on its current customers to better understand the trends of its customers. The market map can then be used as a database of customer information, allowing Spruce to keep it organized in one area.

IX. Appendices

Market map figures

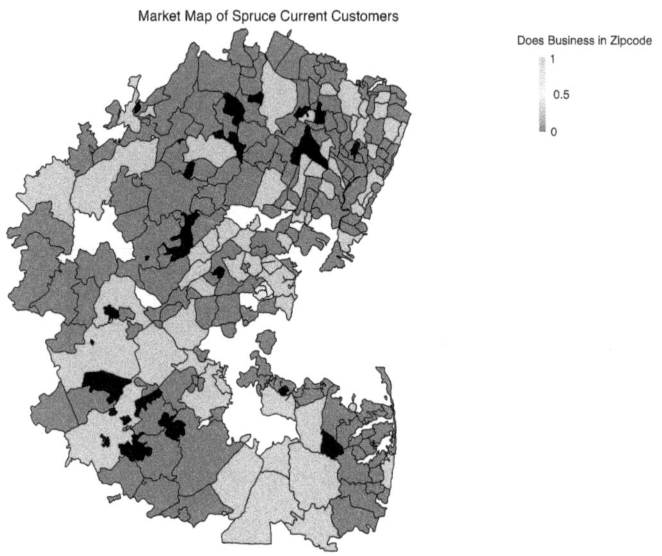

Figure App 2F.5 Market map one.

Figure App 2F.6 Market map two.

Student Count | Teacher Count | Student and Teacher Count | Does Business in Zipcode | Number of schools in district | Maxin Sales

Sort Smallest to Largest
Sort Largest to Smallest
Sort by Color
Clear Filter From "Does Business in ..."
Filter by Color
Number Filters
Search
(Select All)
0
0.5
1
(Blanks)
OK
Cancel

Student Count	Number of schools in district	Maxin Sales
3	64	$ 1
2	39	$
2	36	$
2	51	$
1	19	$
1	26	$
1	14	$
1	17	$
1	6	$
1	11	$
1	18	$
	10	$
	13	$
	17	$
	11	$
	20	$
	15	$
	10	$
	11	$
	11	$

Figure App 2F.7 Spreadsheet example.

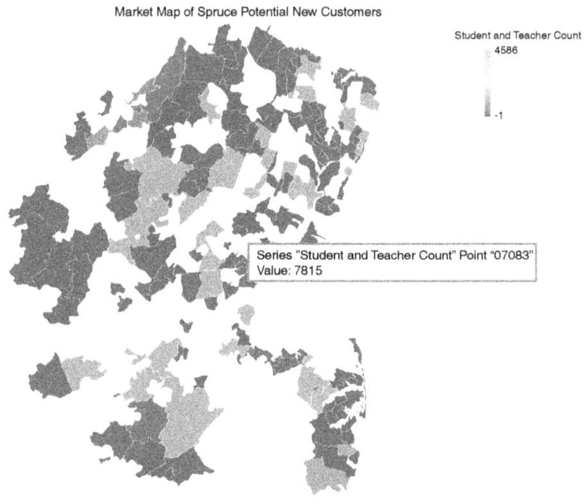

Figure App 2F.8 Potential firms.

District	Town		State	Zipc e
Magic Garden School	Wharton		NJ	08854
Reining In Life Learning Academy	Carteret			08854
New Brunswick Board of Education	New Brunswick		NJ	07102
Rutgers University Healthcare Facilities	Piscataway		NJ	07016
Childhood Dreams Daycare Inc	Northampton		PA	07719
Long Branch Board of Ed	Long Branch		NJ	07103
Berkeley Heights Public School	Berkeley Heights		NJ	08903
Pinelands Regional School Board of Ed	Tuckerton		NJ	08903
Washington Township Bd Of Ed	Long Valley		NJ	08854
New Customer	Ewing		NJ	08648

Figure App 2F.9 List of targets.

References

Administrator. (2020, January). *Welcome to ATRA Janitorial Supply Co., Inc.*, Retrieved from www.atrajanitorialsupply.com/

"Cleaning Tools – Cleaning." *The Home Depot* (2020, January). Retrieved from www.homedepot.com/b/Cleaning-Cleaning-Tools/N-5yc1vZcb51?catStyle=ShowProducts

Cintas (2020). Retrieved March 9, 2020 from www.cintas.com/facilityservices.

"Enlightening Sales Leadership." *Sales Management Association*. Retrieved April 9, 2020 from salesmanagement.org/

"Find a Local Distributor." *SSS | Triple S*. (2020, January). Retrieved from triple-s.com/distributors?field_dis_location_tid=All&zipcode=07065

Imperial Dade. (2020, January). "Imperial Dade." *Imperial Dade*. Retrieved from www.imperialdade.com/

Jordan, J., & Kelly, R. (2015). Companies with a formal sales process generate more revenue. *Harvard Business Review*. Retrieved February 21, 2020 from hbr.org/2015/01/companies-with-a-formal-sales-process-generate-more-revenue

Le, T. (2020, January). US INDUSTRY (NAICS) REPORT 42385 Janitorial equipment supply wholesaling in the US. Retrieved February 10, 2020 from https://athena.rider.edu:3780/download/us/en/industry/950/1/0/pdf

Martin, Steve W. (2017). What top sales teams have in common, in 5 charts. *Harvard Business Review*. Retrieved February 21, 2020 from hbr.org/2015/01/what-top-sales-teams-have-in-common-in-5-charts

National Center of Education Statistics. *Search for public schools – Search results*. Retrieved February 22, 2020 from nces.ed.gov/ccd/schoolsearch/school_list.asp?Search=1&State=34&Zip=07065&Miles=30&SchoolType=4&SpecificSchlTypes=all&IncGrade=-1&LoGrade=-1&HiGrade=-1&SchoolPageNum=2

National Center for Education Statistics. (2020, April). Retrieved from https://nces.ed.gov/ccd/districtsearch/

New Jersey Department of Education. Retrieved February 20, 2020 from https://www.nj.gov/cgi-bin/education/csg/19/csggrsum.pl?string=L.%20ALL&maxhits=10000

"New Jersey Department of Education." (2020, April). *Taxpayers' guide to education spending 2019*. Retrieved from www.nj.gov/education/guide/2019/

"NORTHEAST SUPPLY, INC." (2020, February). *NORTHEAST SUPPLY, INC.* Retrieved from ordernortheast.com/

Plaksji, Z. (2020). Sales process: A structured approach to closing sales faster!" *CRM Blog: Articles, Tips and Strategies by SuperOffice*. Retrieved March 4, 2020 from www.superoffice.com/blog/sales-process/

Root. "Spruce Industries." *SSS | Triple S*, May 1, 2015, triple-s.com/spruce-industries-1. SPRUCE INDUSTRIES: Solutions, Support, Sustainability. (n.d.). Retrieved February 10, 2020 from http://www.spruceindustries.com/index.jsp

"The Original Sales Assessment Company." *Objective Management Group*. Retrieved March 21, 2020 from www.objectivemanagement.com/

Appendix 2G: Final sample project 2

Elite Fashions
Prepared by:
Student A
Student B
Student C
Student D
Under the guidance of:
Dr. Dennis Barber III
Miller School of Entrepreneurship
East Carolina University

Executive summary

East Carolina University's Family Business Management consultants proudly present the following report. Through the past fall 2018 semester, team members XXXXX have worked with Elite Fashions and the Lil Elite Boutique, located in Goldsboro, North Carolina. The company is still owned by its founder, Evelyn Johnson, who now at 80 years old, wishes to retire and give the business to her successor, either Kimberly or Jordan Bogue. The purpose of this report is to outline short-term and long-term goals of the company, identify problems, and provide recommendations on how to achieve the goals and solve the problems.

This report will help with estate and successor planning by choosing a successor and specifically outlining job duties. It will also discuss the benefits of family communication through creating a council and initiating meeting by outlining their importance, no matter the size. In addition, it will discuss the process of creating a buy-sell agreement and the importance of a business valuation. During the semester, Family Business Management consultants met with Dr. Barber to discuss the buy-sell agreement and the business valuation, and the implications they have on Elite Fashions. The end of the report offers the successor a few tips on the proper exit strategy, in case they decide they do not want to run the venture anymore for whatever reason.

Keywords

Estate and Succession Planning; Family Communication; Agreements; Exit Pathway for Successor; and Apartment Capabilities

History of the family business

Downtown Goldsboro, through generations, is a place that has experienced many changes, some good and some bad, but through it all, the community is still dedicated to its development. Traveling on a road called Walnut Street, downtown, one cannot help but notice one prominent building that has stood through the generations, and now houses a 55-year-old unique boutique. Unlike other fashion hubs, this boutique is a cut above the competition, with their competitive advantage of a personalized, dedicated shopping experience and exclusive clothing lines. Once inside the family-owned and family-operated store, also known as "Elite Fashions," customers are warmly greeted by either Evelyn Johnson, the original passionate founder and owner; Chris Etheridge, the vice president, merchandising and account manager; or Jordan Bogue, the youngest family member with a fire for knowledge and entrepreneurship. These three individuals make up the primary employment team for the store's day-to-day operations. Occasionally, Kim Bogue, the Power of Attorney for Evelyn, stops by the store and is happy to help customers if there is a need.

Kim Bogue's husband is currently in landscaping, and she is a full-time employee at Deacon Jones in Greenville. Through networking at their full-time jobs, a lot of business gets referred to Elite Fashions. Their regular clientele is made up of the same people that are local to the area, allowing them to host many events throughout the year like trunk shows, sidewalk sales, and holiday shows, attracting old and new local customers throughout the area. In 2017, Jordan was inspired to open her own boutique within the store, Lil Elite Boutique, targeting her generation for clientele, bringing in a fresh new look and the ability to compete with both trendy and reserved boutiques. Jordan is currently working on updating the websites for both businesses, and she also keeps a social media platform on Facebook and Instagram to help market to more clients that they may not be able to reach otherwise.

After opening Lil Elite Boutique inside of the store, they have noticed an interesting change in how some of their customers shop. The clients for Elite Fashions start getting older as the owner, Evelyn, gets older too, but that does not stop the older generation from buying from the younger generation's store. The older women will end up buying for themselves, their daughters, and their granddaughters at Lil Elite Boutique, and they are satisfied with getting more clothing for less money than they would have otherwise shopping just at the Elite Fashions' portion. Both businesses coincide with one another and complement each other, but as time progresses, the family is approaching a time of decision-making that will best secure the future of both ventures.

Evelyn Johnson, founder and creator of "Elite Fashions," was inspired through her life experiences to take the risk of starting her own company. Marrying at 16 years old to Albert Johnson, she started her life happy, and even found happiness in work with a job in retail. As she matured, she had other jobs, including banking, where she met a friend named Geneva World, and another in retail working for Sears. Evelyn discovered she had a propensity for retail; she loved the community and the fun fashion brought to an environment. One afternoon in Goldsboro, Evelyn was having a cup of coffee with her friend Geneva, when suddenly a building caught their eye. The vacant building was an answer to a question they had not yet asked, and that was "yes, we should open a business," and from there the venture soared. In 1963, an offer was made to purchase the building for well under market value. The offer was accepted, the building was remodeled and stocked, and Elite Fashions opened in the same year the idea was created. The building and business stood strong in the community then, and it continues to hold a strong reputation now.

Like most things in life, Elite Fashions experienced growing pains in 1974, when the partnership between Evelyn and Geneva began to crumble. Evelyn at this time kept the store and transformed the partnership into an c-corporation, where the store experienced taxation twice. After some time, the company would experience another change when it switched again to an s-corporation, being more beneficial for stockholders while avoiding double taxation. Geneva would go on to have three failed businesses, while Evelyn prospered with Elite Fashions. Today, the business is structured with Jordan's new Lil Elite Boutique nestled inside, and with her current bachelor's degree and in-progress master's degree, the succession of Elite Fashions is heading in a positive direction.

The question Kim and Jordan Bogue have now is, what is next? They have no succession plan in writing, and before meeting with them on September 25, 2018, they have not decided on whether they should take care of this now or after Evelyn passes away. The worry is that there are so many people in the family that someone could end up getting their feelings hurt. However, feelings should not be hurt in this case because the only people dealing with the operations are Evelyn, Chris, Kim, and Jordan.

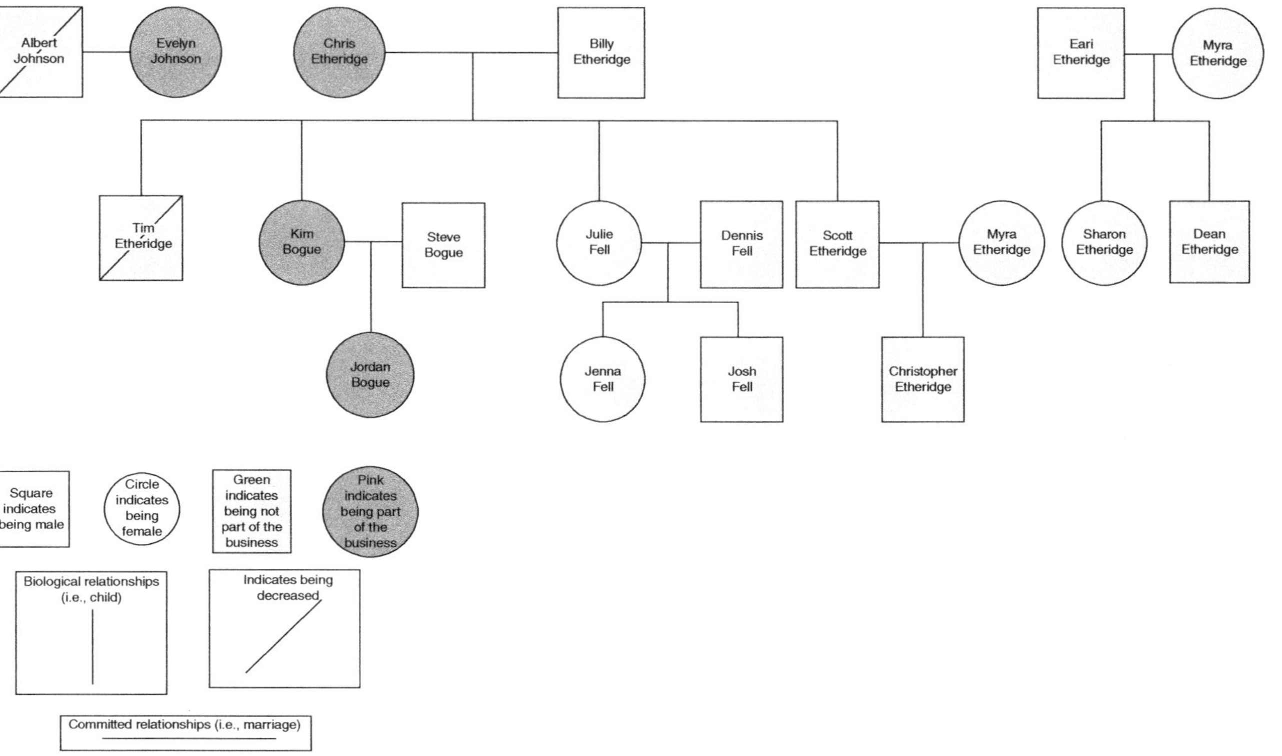

Figure App 2G.1 Genogram and key.

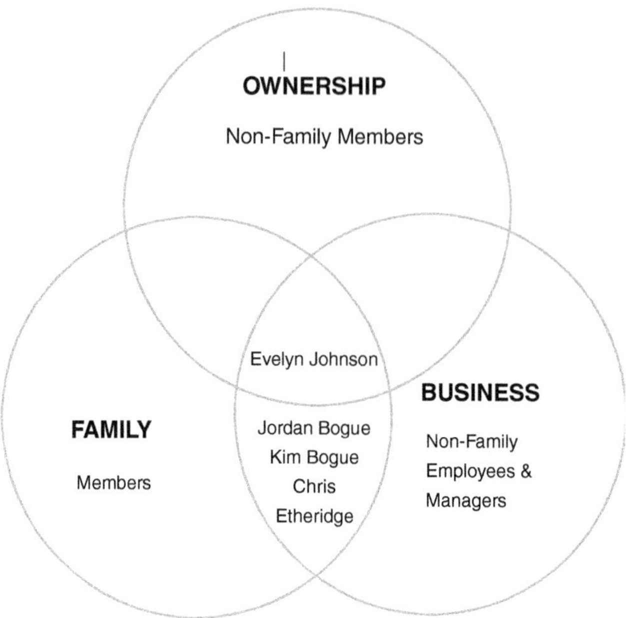

Figure App 2G.2 Systems diagram.

Currently, the only plan for the family is to read the will when Evelyn passes away. The building is owned by Evelyn, and the first floor is used for all their merchandise. The second floor of the building is completely empty, holding old displays and hangers for their store. Downtown Goldsboro is seeing a lot of revitalization, and, next to their store location, apartments are being renovated in a previously abandoned building. They have the option to invest their money/shares in the company after Evelyn's passing and turn the second floor into apartment buildings to follow suit with the other buildings surrounding them. There is also uncertainty about whether or not to keep the two businesses together or to separate them during the succession planning process.

Currently, Lil Elite Boutique is a DBA (doing business under Elite Fashion as its own entity) making it legally a part of the original business, meaning Evelyn has sole ownership of it even though Jordan has started up the company. Jordan has no stock in the businesses, and she would like to continue to keep Lil Elite Boutique even after her great aunt has passed. If everything was left to Jordan, she would keep both businesses alive and together, seeing no reason to rid of a company her aunt and family have spent their lives building.

Family genogram

Based on given information, the Family Business Management consultants have constructed the following family genogram. A genogram is comparable to a family tree, though with more detail, it becomes highly informative. A genogram can capture family events outside of just lineage, such as a divorce, or removal of a cousin. Family businesses operate uniquely from typical corporations, making conflict management more essential (Poza & Daugherty, 2014, p. 39). Some genograms can indicate these shaky relationships within the family when provided enough information. A genogram may indicate family trends, like morals, but illnesses as well, like heart disease and alcoholism. Elite Fashion's genogram seems to indicate that there are multiple family members not related to Evelyn, increasing the risk that one may become greedy regarding the business upon the time of her death. Elite Fashion's Genogram can be seen in Figure App 2G.1.

Systems diagram

The systems theory perspective is a broad, encompassing way of looking at the three elements affecting family firms: family, management, and ownership. All the three elements overlap and are interdependent on one another in some way, thanks to the uniqueness of family firms. By drawing a role systems diagram, the line is drawn separating subsystems. It is important to practice synergy among each element, making the gap flow as smooth as possible. This system is maintained as a dynamic social system, achieving success through reciprocal adjustments between subsystems when necessary (Poza & Daugherty, 2014, p. 9). Elite Fashions systems diagram can be seen in Figure App 2G.2.

Statement of the project objectives

Short-term objectives

The short-term objectives for both boutiques must be fully addressed before the more critical issues can be addressed, pertinent to the business. Currently Jordon is listed as the successor, but multiple variables suggest that Kimberly would be equally qualified, if not more qualified, to run the family business. The family needs to decide who will be the successor. Regardless of who is selected, both family members will still be heavily involved in the business. Roles should be outlined for both the successor and family business member for the future. If Kimberly is selected, a succession plan for Jordan should be outlined to ensure the next succession is even easier and smoother than the last.

Long-term objectives

Once the previously mentioned short-term objectives are satisfied, achieving the long-term objectives should become a simple process. The first major step this boutique must accomplish is physically and legally transferring power, or ownership, through either the will, or a buy-sell agreement. This document outlines each essential component regarding transferring power. A business valuation should be performed on Elite Fashions as they have not had one in years. If Jordan is selected as successor, exit pathways are discussed so she is aware of the best way to leave the business. Finally, a quick note will be made assessing the potential of using the second story for apartments in the future.

Areas of improvement

The consultants in East Carolina University's Family Business Management course believes they can help Elite Fashions improve their process of succession. According to *Family Business* (4th Edition), by Ernesto Poza and Mary Daugherty, family firms are unique because of the way succession plays a key, strategic role in the company's life. "Because competitive success, family harmony, and ownership returns are all at stake at the same time in the firm, carefully orchestrating the multi-year process represented by succession across generations of owner-managers is a priority" (Poza & Daugherty, 2014, p. 8). With poor succession planning, family businesses may find their futures too conservative, rebellious, or wavering. In other words, if they act too conservatively, the firm may be locked in the past, hiding in the shadow of the last leader. Conversely, an overtly rebellious mindset disregards the previous owner's business model, sometimes starting with a clean slate. This risk may cause the company to lose the 'recipe for success,' along with the business's tradition and legacy. With a wavering mindset in a succession plan, the next generation is paralyzed with indecisiveness, often shown by not responding to competitive conditions and opportunities fast enough. The Family Business Management consultants will heed these warnings in the recommendation section of crafting the succession plan for Elite Fashions.

Estate and succession planning

The current plan is to wait until Evelyn's passing and to use the will to transfer power, but according to the book *Family Business*, waiting until death to succeed the business is too risky of a strategy. Outside family members may emerge at the time of her death, demanding an undeserved inheritance, and some are successful at receiving them. Making the decision not to wait until Evelyn passes is a huge area of improvement the company can make.

Succession plans can be created during any stage of the business, but, for Elite Fashions, the creation of this plan will be prioritized over the next year because Evelyn Johnson is in her 80s. This plan will protect the business and the successor, either Kim or Jordan Bogue, from any issues that could arise after Evelyn's passing. Evelyn's will currently states that Jordan can take over Elite Fashions at her death, but there is question about whether Jordan should be the first legal successor. Jordan plans to graduate in December of 2019 with her master's degree. As of right now, she wants to be able to devote all her professional time to the business, but at the age of 19, her mind could change. For that reason, the family is considering transferring power to her mother, Kim, instead, who is slightly more experienced in the company. Once a successor is assigned, the family may begin drafting the next succession plan, using the first one as a model, making improvements along the way. If Kim is selected, creating the succession plan for her daughter should come as a top priority, to allow her to easily legally step into the new leadership role with confidence. Succession is confused as a 'one-day-event,' many times, when in actuality, succession is a process occurring slowly over years. Before Jordan takes on sole responsibility for the company, she must fully understand every aspect of the business, and every job role of the company leader.

Family communication

Based on the Family Business Management's consulting speculation, the business and Evelyn's plans for succession are not being discussed throughout the entire family. Current stock and dealings of the business belong solely in the hands of Evelyn, Chris, Kim, and Jordan. There are a lot of other members in their family, but no one else works or has any interest in Elite Fashions. The issue stated by Kim was that, even though these family members have not invested in the business now, they could want a payout in some form from the business in the future when Evelyn passes. Right now, there is no family council or meetings happening within the business, which could lead to disagreements and family arguments if family members are not informed on what the future holds for Elite Fashion. Family meetings would benefit Elite Fashions because they give everyone a chance to discuss business matters and be transparent with each other (Poza & Daugherty, 2014).

Agreements

Elite Fashions' founder Aunt Evelyn Johnson desires to transfer power to keep the company alive through the generations to her great niece Jordan Bogue. The first step in achieving this goal is to create a buy-sell agreement for both companies, using a business valuation created with an external professional.

Exit pathway for successor

With Jordan as the ideal successor of Elite Fashions, she is assuming vast responsibility while still completing her master's degree. Hesitation lies about who should be the successor, also because of her age and current lack of ties. In the event she gets married later in life, the store may become a burden. There are six common CEO exit styles outlined in *Family Business*, two of which are negative, and the remaining four are positive. The recommendation will explain each in hopes that if the successor decides to leave the venture, they will use one of the methods.

Apartment capabilities

During a client meeting, Kim disclosed that the budget for the second story apartment renovations would equate to $200,000. Depending on the level of need for the upstairs remodel, particularly if there is a need for new drywall and additional wall construction, this estimate may be low. However, if flooring, ceiling fans, bathroom amenities and fixtures, appliances, paint, furniture, cabinets, house wiring, inspection fees, permits, and more are the only concerns, this budget may be achievable.

Below is a list of questions summarizing the problems Elite Fashions and the Lil Elite Boutique are currently facing and are the core areas the Family Business Management consultants hope to address in the following recommendations section. These problems are modeled after the short- and long-term goals discussed in the statement of project objectives.

- Who is better qualified to be selected for successor, Kim or Jordan Bogue?
- Duties and job descriptions outlined for the current CEO and remaining employees to make hiring and retaining the right personnel easier.
- Regardless of successor succession, a successor plan and timeline should be created for the following successor.
- Lacking family communication may be repaired through implementing consistent communication channels, such as a family council or family meetings.
- Elite Fashions has limited knowledge of buy-sell agreements and their benefits.
- Complete a business valuation.
- Jordan or Kim may change their minds about running the business, indicating the need for an exit pathway for the successor.
- Is opening an apartment complex wise?

Recommendations

Throughout the recommendations section of the paper, the Family Business Management consultants will address all of the previous areas of improvement in the following order: estate and succession planning, family communication, agreements: buy-sell agreement, business valuation, exit pathway for the successor, and apartment capabilities. In each element, useful resources are tied in with the recommendation, to create the best value for the client, Elite Fashions and the Lil Elite Boutique.

Make Jordan the successor for Elite Fashions

The Family Business Management consultants would like to offer a recommendation to Elite Fashions about deciding the successor for the company: either Jordan or Kim. After careful consideration, Jordan is the one who can assume the role as the first legal successor to the business. While her age and lack of ties are current hindrances, they can also be viewed as her personal competitive advantage. Young, but intelligent Jordan is no stranger to hard work and will have to be diligent during the transition to not fall behind on school work in her master's program. She must also accept that the business is hers now, and she cannot back-out or run away from it easily, no matter the circumstance, which is likely to change based on her age. Her perseverance to achieve success marks her as a strong leader and an ideal candidate for the succession.

Jordan's creativity, innovativeness, and demographics combine to create sparkling new possibilities for Elite Fashions. For that reason, the Family Business Management consultants want to caution her to remember the importance in also maintaining tradition. "One generation built great business success, and the next one destroyed it. It was not because the latter was lazy or incompetent, but because essential conversations about family business succession sat on the back burner until it was too late" (Clarke, 2018). This quote exemplifies the risk that Elite Fashions has if succession planning is not properly written, understood, and executed.

To assist with planning, the Family Business Management consultants offer five mistakes commonly made in succession planning and how to counteract them. The first mistake lies in lack of time, where not enough time is dedicated to working *on* the business, instead of *in* the business. Through an avenue like monthly family council meetings this can be easily avoided. Next, since succession planning is overwhelmingly complex, many businesses procrastinate the plan until there is no time left. By acting now, as Elite Fashions is doing, and working with East Carolina University's Family Business Management consultants, they are currently preventing this pitfall. Third, "out of 70% of family businesses will fail in their second generation. Of those, 60% attribute their failure to communication woes" (Clarke, 2018). Communication issues are most easily resolved by having a space that does not allow things to reach that point, such as family meetings or council, where family members can hear and be heard. Fourth, interpersonal conflict can cause loyalties to form with certain family members if there is a perceived power divide. For this reason, by outlining job duties, roles are more clearly established, and again, family meetings should prevent this if operating correctly. Finally, CEOs and owners may experience 'the Ostrich Syndrome' where they do not want to admit their time is short or may even push out thoughts of death. The best way to explain this syndrome is with a quote, "rather than face up to the fact that life will go on without them, they bury their head in the sand and carry on without a second thought about the future" (Clarke, 2018).

With Jordan as the next successor of Elite Fashions, there is no immediate rush to begin adjusting the succession plan. However, if Jordan is planning to start her own family in the future, these new additions to the family business would call for an updated, modified succession plan tailored to the next successor.

Recognize successor qualities

Experiencing money management at a young age is the first way to begin developing the success of a family business. *Family Business* outlines the "3+3+3+1=10" Rule, meaning for every $10 earned, $3 should be saved, $3 should be consumed, $3 should be invested in learning a new skill, and $1 should be used for philanthropic purposes. This can also be thought of in terms of percent of profits. Teaching this early to young business family members leads to more financial success in the future. The main point in this example illustrates how training and orienting potential successors' minds from a young age with no chance of bail can prepare them much quicker for real-world responsibilities of the business. This includes keeping everyone informed about major operations, communicated in an age-appropriate manner.

Two attributes researched as most desirable for successors are integrity and commitment. Gardening respect of employees is a close third decided by senior generations. Interestingly, bloodline and technical skills like management and marketing mean little for senior family leaders, as one does not matter and the other can be taught. A better indicator for a good successor would be their attitude and ability to adapt and learn quickly, among other relational personal skills. These are just a few of the important considerations for successor to CEO. Other relative characteristics include competence, followed by decision-making skills and interpersonal skills.

Family Business emphasizes that the successor must be good at decision-making, always putting the company and the family first. If the successor cannot be trusted to make good decisions, then they are not ready to be CEO. All of the previously listed components are required, but trust from the Board and existing leaders can be the "go" or "no-go," on individuals for succession. Jordan should therefore remember the importance of crafting the next succession plan, when a new successor is even an option.

Outline job descriptions

Aside from succession planning, the Family Business Management consultants recommend that the business hierarchy be broken down with clearer roles and duties that will eliminate chance circumstances. For example, if both Jordan and Kim have store-ordering power, they may accidently over-order for the store. The family can outline individual duties, job descriptions, and responsibilities to distribute the workload in a fair manner. They also can create base employment requirements such as education or experience for each job. This way, each job will have minimum requirements and assigned duties, making each role in the company clearer. Through this, if the business ever decides to hire externally, they are now prepared to do so. Often at least one outsider perspective can play a sort of 'devil's advocate' role, allowing for deep, unconventional thinking, indicating that hiring externally can have a positive influence on a family business. These clearly defined roles can even impact the CEO, either strengthening or lightening their workload. The work should be proportionate to the nature of the business and to another employee's workload.

Diversify employment

Elite Fashions can consider hiring at least one non-family member employee to diversify their mindset on any topic and seek expertise in an area they are lacking. Elite Fashions is protected and ready to hire someone externally because of the outlined job descriptions mentioned in the recommendation above.

Create a family council

A family council is a group of family members meeting to discuss current events, policies, products, shareholders, plans, and even the mission statement. They meet regularly as decided per family and prevent family members from feeling ignored as their concerns are addressed during council meetings. They also are emotionally beneficial in this way as worries are communicated and trust and respect are built for each other and the company. Council meetings also reduce the likelihood of zero-sum dynamics occurring as well (Poza & Daugherty, 2014, p. 44). Family councils typically have a wide range of duties or obligations. For starters, they may plan family meetings for the CEO, discuss family issues and business direction while keeping other family members informed, and help the business reach decisions, as a group, increasing goal strength. They can also develop plans and policies to better assist or correct the business, guard against negative family interference, be it legal or emotional through communication avenues, while inspiring loyalty among family shareholders. In large-enough companies, scouting for talent in the family, as well as creating educational events to encourage family involvement and education about the business, like creating social gatherings to stimulate positive family environments, becomes essential (Davis, 2001). In addition, if Elite Fashions creates a family council, they will have the benefit of structure and guidance, even during times of company crisis. Harvard's Business School says that "Family council meetings are a representative group of their members doing planning, creating policies, and strengthening business-family communication and bond" (Davis, 2001).

Conduct at least one family meeting a year

Since the family's communication is lacking, conducting family meetings would be the best way to keep the entire family informed on the direction and plans for the business. Family meetings are not only for the members involved directly in the business but also for any other member who may be curious in how the company is doing. There are many benefits that come from family business meetings, and a few of those are "opening the lines of communication, providing a forum for resolving conflict, and communicating family values to subsequent generations" (Harder, 2004).

These three benefits of family meetings all serve a personal purpose of helping Elite Fashions in the months and years to come. Opening lines of communication will allow Evelyn to discuss what she wants for the company and what the plan for succession will be to all the members in the family, allowing for feedback and commentary of family members. Providing a forum for resolving conflict will allow tension and disagreements within the family, regarding the business, to be discussed openly with the entire family's involvement. Communicating family values to further generations will keep the current successor and future successors knowledgeable about the history of the company. Evelyn and her partner Chris have worked very hard to make Elite Fashions a fun, family-friendly environment to the downtown

Goldsboro area, and it is important that the generations that follow them understand that the future success of this business is dependent on keeping the company's culture and values intact.

Family meetings "can strengthen their families, the business, and the succession planning process" (Harder, 2004). *Family Business* warns about family relations and zero-sum dynamics, describing this as when one party feels like their loss is the victor's win. The main benefit family meetings bring is preventing conflict through the constant, regular communication. Meetings can consist of family owners, managers, stakeholders, and even future-generation family members. Meetings are a good way to distribute information about the business, "from the horse's mouth," and can include financial performance, strategies, competitive environment, responsibilities, returns, risk tolerance levels, and more. The goal should be educating and communicating to the weakest informed links, and note, this is not decision time. In addition, this keeps shareholders informed while motivating and increasing the general sense of family respect, trust, and unity. A synergy forms with members after working together for many years. The meetings still allow for new and different perspectives to be presented to the business.

Elite Fashions may therefore hold annual family meetings, open to all family members. As many are not interested in the business, they may or may not attend, but simply by extending the offer to family relations who are slightly better off. If at some point the company would like to sell stock, family members will likely be the first purchasers, and as stakeholders, deserve to be informed therefore requiring family meetings. This in the future could be a great opportunity to host a social gathering for the family to increase involvement and improve family relations. At a minimum, the family meetings will generate more interest and pride in the family legacy.

Aside from one annual family meeting, the family council can meet once a month, or at bare minimum, quarterly, to discuss any relevant matters. Through these constant meetings, innovation will be sparked in Elite Fashions and the Lil Elite Boutique as communication can go off openly and smoothly. In the event the decision is made to go ahead and renovate the upstairs living area, family meetings become an even larger must. Construction sounds, potential messes, potential complaints, and hazards will put a lot of stress on the relationship of the new adjusting CEO and employees. Without a clear line of communication, this area may become a breeding ground for conflict.

Create a buy-sell agreement

Buy-sell agreements are contractual agreements between shareholders and the company. Buy-sell agreements are important because families can maintain some form of role in the company financially while being free to pursue other ventures. Shareholders in some cases are given liquidity options and can buy out of the company. This can be done with dividends, buy-sell agreements, and fund redemption. This in a way gives companies the competitive advantage being able to maintain concentrated ownership and family control. One final note is that buy-sell agreements have risk management constraints. For example, for stock to be redeemed for the year, the company must be over the 'safe money amount limit' if you will, as backup, for the company. Then, they can be redeemed (Poza & Daugherty, 2014, p. 70).

According to licensed attorney Priyanka Prakash on *fitsmallbusiness.com*, a buy-sell agreement has three key benefits: It keeps the business in the right hands, it defines when you can sell your part of the business and to whom, and finally it specifies a fair price for the business. Prakash describes four types of buy-sell agreements on her website, which is included in the references page. For now, we are going to focus on the one that applies most to Elite Fashions: The One-Way Buy-Sell Plan.

The One-Way Buy-Sell Plan occurs when a sole proprietor such as Aunt Evelyn desires to succeed the business after death or disability to a child, or key employee, both of which describe her grandniece Jordan, or even a spouse. The main component in this is that the child would buy an insurance policy on the owner and be the beneficiary of the policy, either paying the premiums personally, or allowing the business to pay them. One-Way Buy-Sell Plans are ideal for family-run businesses who are dependent on a key employee, as Elite Fashions is with the successor Jordan, allowing her specifically to succeed the business. This can also be useful for Evelyn, so she can retire from the business, rather than die in the role of CEO.

This creates the opportunity for Jordan to get term life insurance on Aunt Evelyn, using the cash value built up in the policy to buy out the owner's share when she retires. The four main components of the buy-sell agreement are the trigger events, buyout structure, value of the business, and how the agreement will be funded, with insurance or some other way (Prakash, 2017). To complete the buy-sell agreement for Elite Fashions, the Family Business Management consultants met with Jordan to go through the process and discuss the different implications of each choice, using the template on *fitsmallbusiness.com* (see Appendix A for the buy-sell agreement).

Elite Fashions must decide how to fund the buy-sell agreement and can do so with any of the following sources: cash, loans, life insurance, disability insurance, installment sales, permanent life insurance policy, stock options, or deferred compensation arrangements. Most commonly, businesses chose the life insurance option, because it "provides security and assurance that the benefits will be paid as specified in the contract for a pre-determined cost" (Prakash, 2017). With Elite Fashion's One-Way Buy-Sell Agreement, Jordan would buy a life insurance policy on Aunt Evelyn, which could be term or permanent life insurance. In their circumstance, the Family Business Management consultants believe the term life insurance is better suited for their needs, as it is most affordable, covering Evelyn for a specific time period, needing renewal. With her age and transferring power to Jordan, the benefits of a permanent life insurance policy are lost.

The Family Business Management consultants want to next warn Elite Fashions of the pitfalls of this agreement, being that insurance is key, and an inadequate policy can spell trouble in future generations. In addition, the successor may not be able to pay for the insurance premiums, leaving it as a business expense. This is acceptable depending on how the payments are characterized; as a bonus or loan of the premiums, or as a 'lease' of the death benefits. Be careful, here the premiums may or may not be deductible to the business, increasing business taxes, the very aspect Elite Fashions wishes to avoid. The buy-sell agreement can be difficult to fill out without a lawyer present (see Appendix B for a walk-through on the buy-sell agreement).

Have an external business valuation conducted

Business valuations are extremely appreciated in families in private businesses, as they identify an updated, fair price for the business using one of two methods: their own calculations using the valuation formula or hiring an external professional appraisal team. Using the valuation formula, Elite Fashions can appraise themselves based on their seller discretionary earnings, or SDE, over more common book values like net earnings or business revenues. SDE is the business's earnings plus nonrecurring or irregular expenses, multiplied by an industry multiple, to equate the value of the business (Prakash, 2017). The SDE and industry multiple should be updated annually to avoid disagreements over fair valuation practices. For assistance in calculating this, the article provides step-by-step instructions and can be found in the references. Alternatively, for an estimated $2,000–$5,000, Elite Fashions can hire a third party to perform the business valuation.

The business valuation should be included in the buy-sell agreement and outline the sale specifics, like if just the physical aspects are included, or assets and debts, or if commercial real estate is included, as would be with Elite Fashions. By including the business valuation in the agreement, the owner has the luxury of having control over what the business is worth. The IRS will use whatever value given within reason for estate valuation, but without one provided, the IRS creates one for the business, sometimes dropping the value.

Select the ambassador exit style

Family Business outlines six common exit styles of CEOs from the business: monarch, general, ambassador, governor, inventor, and transition czar. For convenience, the list of common CEO exit styles has been created below, outlining briefly each exit style and its characteristics.

Monarch CEO who considers themselves immortal. They never plan to move power and want to go out as CEO. Resistant to change and growth, they often fire many individuals and keep younger generations out of top management. Consequently, as a result of the secrets, the recipe for success is often lost. This typically generates a greedy family after the CEO passes as well.

General These leaders are similar to monarchs, in that they never want to leave. Once they do, you will likely find them enjoying retirement, waiting for a notice that the successor made a huge mistake, and they need to come back. Family with this exit style should enjoy leaving while they can.

Ambassador Ambassador leaders make excellent board members after leaving the company because they trained and selected the next family and nonfamily leaders. Ambassadors are marked by exiting slowly to ensure the new leaders are prepared.

Governor These CEOs commit themselves to leaving in a certain timeframe or date. This ensures the succession plan is in motion, as it drives production in meeting the deadlines to secure sustainability and continuity.

Inventor Marked by creative CEOs who exit one company to enter as CEO in another.

Transition Czar Transition Czars typically partner with their spouse to create a new system for remaining workers, actively including family, nonfamily, managers, customers, and suppliers in the succession and continuity process.

Based on this information, Elite Fashions can consider these six exit styles, with ambassador, governor, inventor, and transition czar being more business-positive. It is our recommendation that when it comes time for Evelyn to exit the business, she operates as an ambassador. Exiting as an ambassador will allow a thorough planning process for Elite Fashions, while increasing communication between Evelyn and Jordan and decreasing any interpersonal conflicts that could occur with the complexity of the exiting process. Evelyn started this company from the ground up, which makes her the ideal board member after selling her ownership to Jordan.

Seek further recommendations from another course

With competition for living space increasing in the area, Elite Fashions wants to consider opening their own apartments above the store's location. This may provide a trendy competitive advantage, as leasers can say they uniquely live on top of a boutique, giving downtown Goldsboro a swanky new living area. However, the Family Business Management consultants caution the business with this idea and would like Elite Fashions to consider the following questions: How will renters enter and exit the building? What happens in the event a tenant wanders into the store in leisure home wear, affecting the store's image? Is the new successor ready for these challenges or should the renovator Kim assume the legal roles? These are a few examples, but these and more are the questions that must be answered in this brainstorming phase.

Financially speaking, to remodel six full apartments, $200,000 is a bit of a low-end budget. To be competitive with the new location opening, Elite Fashions cannot simply offer living space but must offer an atmosphere or amenities above that of the competition, unless they are comfortable with being associated as the cheaper option. Considering the company is currently branded as an elitist fashion hub, competing on price may inevitably hurt this strong brand image. Therefore, the estimated $200,000 should be raised to $300,000, allowing the company more freedom in renovating the apartments.

Our brief recommendation to Elite Fashions would be to refurbish the second story to be a place of class and quality to match their brand image, using careful planning and budgeting before initializing this process. With the succession underway, focusing solely on the apartments may prove trying, so a timeline lasting up to five years can be drafted, outlining individual steps along the way for the renovation process. If planned correctly, all of the apartments can undergo the same maintenance and services at the same time, reducing cost and the number of times a service provider will be used. Through this planning, the goal is likely obtainable within three to five years, allowing for Elite Fashions to generate even more profit long term, while expanding their company. Since the apartments are not necessarily a family management matter for our course, the College of Business could point Elite Fashions to another management course for further recommendations and details on the apartment capabilities.

Conclusion and comments

After months of dedication, meetings, and communication, East Carolina University's Family Business Management consultants are proud to present this report to Elite Fashions and the Lil Elite Boutique. The recommendations cover estate and succession planning, family communication, buy-sell agreements, business valuation, exit pathways for the successor, and apartment capabilities.

With Jordan as successor, and five pitfalls outlined, success can be easily obtained for both business ventures. The next steps in succession planning will involve considering adjustments for future successors and refining the business roles and job duties.

Following this, a family council should be created, no matter how small, that meets monthly to discuss any relevant business information ranging from its sale to quarterly promotions. The open line of communication will improve the synergy from employee to CEO. Annual family meetings open to external family members may also be conducted to raise interest and earn family support for business operations.

The Agreements section covers two key aspects for their succession plan: the buy-sell agreement and the business valuation. For the buy-sell agreement the Family Business Management consultants agree that the One-Way Buy-Sell Plan is the best fitting for Elite Fashions, allowing Jordan to fund the business purchase through being the beneficiary of Evelyn's term life insurance policy, either under her own buying power or the company's. The agreement will be funded using a term life insurance policy on Aunt Evelyn.

Also, for the buy-sell agreement, a business valuation is needed, which can be calculated using seller discretionary earnings or SDE. This can be figured either using *fitsmallbusiness.com's* calculator or hiring an external company. For pricing sake, the valuation was calculated with the team's construction of the buy-sell agreement.

If in the event after succession, Jordan changes her mind, she has already been suggested the exit strategies of either ambassador, governor, or transition czar, allowing for thorough, smart planning, increasing interpersonal relationships so the business can live on.

Last, in the near future, Elite Fashions may consider expanding their renovation budget to create more luxurious apartments than the competition and advertise themselves as a swanky apartment complex above their trendy boutique. Once the details of clientele and store relations are decided and put into writing, and a full budget and plan of action is developed, the company will be ready to begin renovations.

Through consulting Elite Fashions and the Lil Elite Boutique, East Carolina University's Family Business Management's young professional consultants have learned and put to practice invaluable real-world knowledge about managing and succeeding a family business. From the bottom of our hearts, we would like to thank you for trusting us with your private company information, allowing us to exercise recently acquired skills in a highly relevant manner. This has been a pleasure, and as an East Coast pirate family, we wish Elite Fashions and the Lil Elite Boutique success in all their business ventures.

References

Clarke, R. (2018, November 7). The 5 mistakes family business owners are making – Real business. *Real Business*. Retrieved from www.realbusiness.co.uk/five-mistakes-family-business-owners-are-making/

Davis, John A. (2001, November 12). The three components of family governance. *HBS Working Knowledge*. Retrieved from www.hbswk.hbs.edu/item/the-three-components-of-family-governance

Harder, Mark K. (2004, March 5). Using family meetings in your family business succession plan. *Warner, Norcross & Judd*. Retrieved from www.wnj.com/Publications/Using-Family-Meetings-In-Your-Family-Business

Poza, E. J., & Daugherty, M. S. (2014). *Family business*. Mason, OH: South-Western Cengage Learning.

Prakash, P. (2017, July 12). *Buy sell agreement – Why you need one, template, and what to include*. Retrieved from https://fitsmallbusiness.com/buy-sell-agreement/

Appendix A

A rough-draft buy-sell agreement for Elite Fashions and the Lil Elite Boutique

BUY-SELL AGREEMENT

This Buy-Sell Agreement (this "**Agreement**") is made effective as of January 01, 2019 (the "Effective Date"), between and among Elite Fashions and Lil Elite Boutique (the "**Company**") and each of the individuals listed on the attached **Schedule A** (each an "**Owner**," and collectively, the "**Owners**").

The Owners own all of the outstanding common stock of the Company (the "**Units**"), and desire to promote and protect their mutual interests and the interests of the Company. Therefore, the parties hereby agree as follows.

Article I – sales and transfers

1. General Transfer Restriction. No Owner (or any party acting on behalf of an Owner) may sell or transfer any of such Owner's Units, whether now owned or later acquired, except in accordance with the terms of this Agreement or by the written consent of the Company and all of the other Owners. Any attempted sale or transfer of any Units (or any interest in any Units) that violates the terms of this Agreement shall be void and shall not be binding upon, or recognized by, the Company or the Owners.
   a. Sale or Transfer Defined. The phrase "sale or transfer" includes any sale, pledge, encumbrance, gift, bequest, or other transfer of any Units, whether or not the transfer would be made (i) for value, or (ii) to another Owner, or (iii) voluntarily or involuntarily or by operation of law, or (iv) during an Owner's lifetime or upon an Owner's death.
   b. Sale or Transfer Exception. The phrase "sale or transfer" does not include Owner's transfer into a self-settled trust for estate planning purposes.
2. Permitted Voluntary Sale or Transfer During Lifetime. Any Owner who wishes to sell or transfer such Owner's Units must first provide written notice of such intent to each of the other Owners. Such Owner (a "**Seller**") shall be deemed to have offered to sell his/her Units (the "**Offered Units**") to the other Owners. The notice must state the name of the party (the "**Third Party Purchaser**") to whom the Seller wishes to sell or transfer the Offered Units and the terms of the proposed sale or transfer.

a. First Option to Other Owners. Each of the other Owners shall have thirty (30) days from the effective date of the notice during which such other Owners may elect to buy the Offered Units in proportion to their respective ownership of all outstanding Units (excluding the Offered Units) or in such other proportion upon which the other Owners may agree. During this 30-day period, the other Owners must collectively agree to buy all or none of the Offered Units. If the other Owners exercise their option to buy, then they shall acquire the Offered Units on the same terms and conditions as contained in the notice of the proposed sale or transfer, or the pre-determined purchase price as stipulated in Article II, whichever is lower. These terms shall be supplemented as necessary by the payment terms described in Article III below.

b. Permitted Sale or Transfer to Third Party Purchaser. If the other Owners do not validly exercise their option to buy all of the Offered Units within the 30-day period, then the Seller may complete the sale or transfer to the Third Party Purchaser, upon majority approval of the other Owners. However, the sale or transfer must be made on the same terms and conditions as those contained in the notice to the other Owners. Further, the Third Party Purchaser must agree in writing to be bound by the terms of this Agreement, and be limited to 60 percent management control in the operation of the business, before or at the time of the sale or transfer. If the sale or transfer to the Third Party Purchaser is not completed within sixty (60) days after the expiration of the other Owners' 30-day option period, then the authorization under this Agreement for such sale or transfer shall be deemed withdrawn as if no such sale or transfer had been contemplated and no notice had been given.

3. Involuntary Lifetime Disposition/Termination of Employment. Any Owner with knowledge of a possible Involuntary Lifetime Disposition (defined below) must promptly provide written notice to each of the other Owners describing the nature and details of the Involuntary Lifetime Disposition, as well as each involved party (the "**Third Party Transferee**"). The Owner shall be deemed to have offered to sell such Owner's Units (the "**Offered Units**") to the other Owners.

   a. Involuntary Lifetime Disposition. An "**Involuntary Lifetime Disposition**" occurs when an Owner's Units, or any portion or interest in them, are involuntarily sold, transferred, or otherwise disposed of, or an involuntary sale, transfer, or disposal is threatened by any third person, whether by (i) sale upon the execution or in foreclosure of any pledge, hypothecation, lien, or charge, or (ii) acquisition of an interest in such Units by a trustee in bankruptcy or a receiver, or (iii) any other means (but not including the death of the Owner or any purchase by the Other Owners pursuant to the other sections of this Agreement), or (iv) court adjudication of Owner incompetency, or (v) the appointment of a guardian or conservator for an Owner (unless the Owner is a Disabled Employee, as defined below in Article I(4)(a), or (vi) a court order denying the Owner sole ownership of the Owner's Units in connection with a property division in a divorce proceeding.

b. First Option to Other Owners. Each of the other Owners shall have thirty (30) days from the effective date of such notice during which such other Owners must elect to buy the Offered Units in proportion to their respective ownership of all outstanding Units (excluding the Offered Units) or in such other proportion upon which the other Owners agree. Such other Owners shall acquire such Units at the purchase price and on the payment terms described in Articles II and III below.

4. Termination of Employment. If any Owner is employed by the Company (an "**Employee-Owner**") and ceases to be an employee of the Company because the Employee-Owner is a Disabled Employee (see below), or for any other reason, then such Owner shall be deemed to have offered to sell all of his or her Units (the "**Offered Units**") to the Other Owners for the Purchase Price and on the Payment Terms described in Articles II and III below. Further, each other Owner shall agree to buy all of the Offered Units of the selling Employee-Owner in proportion to his or her respective ownership of all outstanding Units (excluding the Offered Units), or in such other proportion upon which the other Owners may agree. Such offer shall be deemed made on the date such Employee-Owner ceased to be an employee of the Company. This provision does not apply to early retirement as discussed below.

a. Disabled Employee. An Employee-Owner is a "**Disabled Employee**" when such person is (i) under a legal decree of incompetency, or (ii) eligible for benefits for more than 50 percent disability under any group or individual disability insurance policy (as confirmed by an insurance company), or (iii) unable to perform substantially all of his or her regular duties for a period which is reasonably expected to last at least 180 substantially consecutive days, as determined by an examining physician, to which examination each Employee-Owner hereby consents.

b. Early Retirement. If the Employee-Owner voluntarily retires prior to age 65 (Family decision) years, or if the Employee-Owner has not given the Company at least five (5) years' prior written notice of his or her intention to leave the Company's employ, the Purchase Price shall be reduced by 0 percent from the amount otherwise determined in Article II below.

5. Death of an Owner. Upon the death of an Owner, his or her Personal Representative (see paragraph 4.a below) will immediately be deemed to have offered to sell to the other Owners all of the deceased Owner's Units (the "**Offered Units**") at the Purchase Price and on the Payment Terms described in Articles II and III below. Each such other Owner shall accept such offer and agree to buy such Offered Units in proportion to his or her respective ownership of all outstanding Units (excluding the Offered Units), or in such other proportion upon which the other Owners may agree. Notwithstanding the actual closing date specified in Article III, Section 2, the transfer of the Units shall be deemed effective at the close of business day of the deceased Owner's death.

   a. Personal Representative. A Seller's "**Personal Representative**" includes any administrator, personal representative, executor, or trustee who has legal responsibility for managing and disposing of the Seller's Units. It also includes any person who succeeds in interest to such Units, if no such fiduciary has control over such Units.

6. Option of the Company. The other Owners shall have the option to transfer their collective purchase rights under Sections 2, 3, 4, and 5 of this Article I to the Company. The Company shall be bound by the time periods set forth above, the purchase price provisions of Article II, and the payment provisions of Article III. The Company may acquire such amounts of life insurance on the lives of the Owners as it deems appropriate to enable it to purchase Offered Units. The option created under this paragraph may be exercised by a consent to transfer signed by Owners who hold at least 75 (Family decision) percent of the outstanding Units.

Article II – purchase price

The "**Purchase Price**" shall be determined in accordance with the provisions of this Article II, and the payment terms are set forth in Article III.

1. Fair Market Value/Purchase Price. The "**Purchase Price**" shall be a pro-rata share of the "**Fair Market Value of the Company**," based on the ratio of the Offered Units to the total number of Units owned by all of the Owners. The Fair Market Value of the Company shall be $0.00, unless otherwise adjusted in accordance with this Article II.
2. Annual Revisions. Each year the Owners shall meet and review the Fair Market Value of the Company. If the Owners unanimously agree, they shall restate the Fair Market Value of the Company to reflect what they believe to be the then current fair market value. Such restated value shall be recorded on a form dated and signed by each Owner and attached to this Agreement. Such restated value shall be effective upon the date last signed by the Owners, or as the Owners otherwise provide.
3. Appraised Value. If for any reason the Owners have not unanimously agreed to an adjustment in the Fair Market Value of the Company on or before the 75th day after the end of a fiscal year, then the Fair Market Value of the Company shall be determined by an appraisal. This determination shall be made as of the date of any deemed offer.
    a. Determination of Appraised Value. The Fair Market Value of the Company shall be determined in the same manner that fair market value would be calculated for federal estate tax purposes if the Seller had died on the date of any deemed offer. However, the calculation shall ignore any alternate valuation date (under IRC Section 2032) or special use valuation (under IRC Section 2032A). Further, the calculation shall ignore any discounts for lack of marketability or minority interest.

1. Mutual Agreement by Owners. The Fair Market Value of the Company shall be the calculation of value that is mutually agreed upon by the Seller and the other Owners.
2. Qualified Appraisers. If the Seller and the other Owners are unable to agree on the calculation of the Fair Market Value of the Company by the twentieth (20th) day prior to the closing (as provided in Article III, Section 2) (the "**Determination Date**"), then the Fair Market

Value of the Company will be determined by one or more independent appraisers who have professional expertise and experience in valuing businesses in the same industry as the Company ("**Qualified Appraisers**").

i. The Seller (individually) and the other Owners (as a group) will each have the opportunity to appoint a Qualified Appraiser within five calendar days following the Determination Date.
ii. If either party fails to appoint a Qualified Appraiser within this five-day period, the other Qualified Appraiser shall unilaterally establish the Fair Market Value of the Company by a written opinion.
iii. If both parties appoint Qualified Appraisers within this five-day period, these two Qualified Appraisers shall establish the Fair Market Value of the Company in a single written opinion agreed to by both of them.
iv. If these two Qualified Appraisers cannot agree on the Fair Market Value of the Company within ten days after the appointment of the latter of them, then these two appointed Qualified Appraisers shall together appoint a third Qualified Appraiser whose sole written opinion shall establish the Fair Market Value of the Company.

3. Delayed Closing Date. The closing date shall be delayed as reasonably necessary in order for the Qualified Appraisers to establish the Fair Market Value of the Company.
4. Majority Action of Other Owners. Any action to be taken by the Company under this section shall be taken by a majority of the Owners, except that the Seller shall not vote directly or indirectly with respect to such actions.

b. Costs. The fees and reimbursed expenses charged by each Qualified Appraiser shall be the obligation of the party who selected that Qualified Appraiser (apportioned among the other Owners, as to the Qualified Appraiser selected by the other Owners). If it becomes necessary to appoint a third Qualified Appraiser, the cost of such third Qualified Appraiser shall be shared equally between the Seller and the other Owners.
c. Cooperation by the Company. The Company will provide the Company's information to the Qualified Appraiser(s) as may be reasonably necessary or useful to determine the Fair Market Value of the Company.

Article III – payment terms

1. Type of Payment. The Purchase Price paid for the Offered Units of a deceased Owner shall be paid in (Family decision) to the extent of the face amount of the life insurance policies that any Owner buying such Units has maintained under Article V of this Agreement. The remaining portion of the Purchase Price shall be paid in check. However, at the option of each other Owner, the remaining portion may be paid in sixty (60) equal monthly installments of principal and interest. Such installment payments shall begin on the date of the closing and shall include interest compounded annually at the prime rate as listed in the *Wall Street Journal* on such closing date. Each other Owner shall give the Seller a negotiable promissory note as evidence of this debt. Such note shall permit the other Owner to prepay all or any part of the principal balance of the note at any time without penalty or premium. Payments shall first be applied to interest. In the event of an inter vivos transaction, the other Owners may exercise their option to buy the Offered Units from the Seller with a down payment of $0.00 of the Purchase Price, with consecutive equal monthly installment payments for 0 months, due and payable on the first day of each month following the exercise of this option by the other Owners, at a 0 percent rate of interest.
2. The Closing. The purchase of the Offered Units will take place at a closing at the Company's primary place of business or at any other place and time to which the parties agree. In the case of the death or voluntary retirement of the Seller, the closing shall be held 180 days after the date of the Owner's death or the effective date of retirement. In all other cases, the closing shall be held within 30 days after the date on which (i) the last option to buy is exercised or lapses, or (ii) the other Owners last become obligated to buy.

   a. Delivery of Certificates. At the closing, the other Owners will pay for the Offered Units. The Seller will deliver certificates representing all of the Offered Units, duly endorsed, free and clear of all encumbrances, and with evidence of payment of all necessary transfer taxes and fees.
   b. Power of Attorney. Each Owner hereby appoints the Company, through its Secretary, as his or her agent and attorney-in-fact to

execute and deliver all documents needed to convey his or her Units, if such selling Owner is not present at the closing. This power of attorney is coupled with an interest and does not terminate on the Owner's disability or death, and continues for as long as this Agreement is in effect, so long as the Owner was mentally capable of consenting, and consented, to the transaction, prior to their disability, incapacitation, or death.

c. Death-Tax Liability. In the case of a sale because of the Seller's death, then notwithstanding any other provision of this Agreement to the contrary, payment for the Offered Units shall not be required until the Personal Representative of the Seller provides a release or other assurances to the reasonable satisfaction of the other Owners that the other Owners are protected from any liability for death taxes related to the Offered Units.
d. Escrow of Units. If any portion of the Purchase Price is evidenced by a promissory note, the certificate(s), if any, for such portion or all of the Offered Units shall be endorsed in blank, or accompanied by a duly executed, blank stock power, and delivered, in escrow, to an entity which customarily acts as an escrow agent. The escrow agent shall hold such documents as security for repayment of the promissory note. Upon notice from the other Owners that the promissory note has been paid in full, the escrow agent shall deliver all deposited certificate(s), if any, to the appropriate other Owners.

Article IV – endorsement of certificates

Endorsement. Promptly after the date each Owner becomes a party to this Agreement, each Owner shall deliver to the Company's secretary all of his or her certificates. The Company's Secretary shall endorse them as follows:

The sale, assignment, transfer, pledge, or other disposition of the Units represented by this Certificate is restricted by the provisions of a buy-sell agreement dated January 01, 2019, as amended from time to time, by and among the Owners of Elite Fashions and Lil Elite Boutique (the "Company"), and with the Company's consent, a copy of which is on file in the Company's office.

Article V – life insurance

1. Required Policies. Each Owner will apply for, own, and be the beneficiary of one or more life insurance policies, one policy on the life of each other Owner. Each policy shall have death proceeds payable in an amount that is the greater of (i) the amount reasonably calculated to fully pay for such beneficiary-Owner's prorata share of the insured-Owner's Units at the Purchase Price, as if the insured-Owner died, or (ii) the amount listed on Schedule B. Each Owner will take any actions required to maintain in force all of the insurance policies that he or she is required to maintain under this Article, and will not cancel them or allow them to lapse without the prior written consent of each other Owner. All dividends on such policies shall be applied to the payment of premiums.
2. Premiums. Each Owner must pay every life insurance premium required under this Article and must give each other Owner proof of such payment within 15 days of the premium due date. Upon failure to provide such proof, any other Owner may pay the premium and be reimbursed by the nonpaying Owner.

Article VI – terminating or amending the agreement

1. Termination. This Agreement will terminate if the Company is dissolved, put into receivership, or becomes bankrupt. Further, Owners who hold at least 80 percent of the outstanding Units may agree in writing to terminate this Agreement. However, the Owners may not voluntarily terminate this Agreement to the disadvantage of any Owner whose Units have been offered (or deemed offered) for sale, but for which the closing date has not yet occurred.
2. Amendment. This Agreement may be amended upon the written consent of Owners who hold at least 80 percent of the outstanding Units. However, the Owners may not amend this Agreement to the disadvantage of any Owner whose Units have been offered (or deemed offered) for sale, but for which the closing date has not yet occurred.

Article VII – continuation of restrictions

This Agreement shall continue to apply to the Units which are the subject of a sale or transfer and to new Units issued by the Company. The transferee shall execute a counterpart signature page to this Agreement. Such signature shall be binding on all Owners and the Company as if the transferee was an original signor.

Article VIII – miscellaneous

1. Tax Status. If at any time the Company has elected a status for tax purposes that is valid only if the owners are individuals or other types of specified entities, then in order to protect such election, no Owner may sell or transfer any of his or her Units to any person if such sale or transfer might reasonably be expected to result in a termination of such election. No attempted sale or transfer in violation of this paragraph will be valid or recognized by the Company.
2. Binding Effect. This Agreement is binding on and enforceable by and against the parties, their successors, legal representatives, heirs, and assigns.
3. Governing Law. This Agreement will be governed by and construed according to the laws of the State of North Carolina.
4. Severability. If any provision of this Agreement is held to be invalid or unenforceable for any reason, the remaining provisions shall continue to be valid and enforceable. If a court finds that any provision of this Agreement is invalid or unenforceable, but that by limiting such provision it would become valid and enforceable, then such provision shall be deemed to be written, construed, and enforced as so limited.
5. Notices. All notices required or permitted to be given under this Agreement must be given in writing and will be deemed given when personally delivered or on the third day after mailing by U.S. registered or certified mail, postage prepaid, with return receipt requested. Notice to any Owner is valid if sent to him or her at such Owner's address as it appears in the Company's records.
6. Specific Performance. The Owners agree that the Units are unique and that the failure to perform the obligations under this Agreement will result in irreparable damage to the other parties. Further, the Owners

agree that specific performance of these obligations may be obtained by a lawsuit in equity.

7. Waiver. Any party's failure to insist on compliance or enforcement of any provision of this Agreement shall not affect its validity or enforceability or constitute a waiver of future enforcement of that provision or of any other provision of this Agreement.
8. Entire Agreement. This Agreement constitutes the entire agreement of the Owners among themselves or with the Company regarding the subject matter of this Agreement and supersedes all prior agreements regarding such subject matter.
9. Effectiveness. This Agreement shall become effective when signed by all of the Owners listed on **Schedule A** and by Evelyn Johnson, CEO, on behalf of Elite Fashions and Lil Elite Boutique.

____

Evelyn Johnson

Elite Fashions and Lil Elite Boutique

By: ____

Evelyn Johnson
CEO

SCHEDULE A

List of Owners
Evelyn Johnson

SCHEDULE B

Name of Each Owner and Life Insurance Policy Amount

Name of Owner	**Amount of Policy**
________________________________	$0.00

References

B2B International. What is the value proposition canvas? Talk to the research experts. Retrieved January 10, 2020 from https://www.b2binternational.com/research/methods/faq/what-is-the-value-proposition-canvas/.

Bozeman, B., & Sweeney, M. K. (2007). Toward a useful theory of mentoring: A conceptual analysis and critique. *Administration & Society, 39*(6), 719–739.

Brownell, J., & Jameson, D. A. (2004). Problem-based learning in graduate management education: An integrative model and interdisciplinary application. *Journal of Management Education, 28*(5), 558–577.

Cherrington, J. O. (1995). Professional attributes for consultants. In *Handbook of management consulting services*. New York: McGraw-Hill.

Ferrell, O. C., & Hartline, M. D. (2016). *Marketing strategy: Text and cases* (6th ed.). Mason, OH: South-Western Cengage Learning.

Gill, T., Heermans, K., & Herath, R. (1998). Puzzled about teams, a handbook. Retrieved June 5, 2003 from http://www.inov8.psu.edu/toolbox/PuzzledAboutTeams.pdf, p. 6.

Godfrey, P. C., Illes, L. M., & Berry, G. R. (2005). Creating breadth in business education through service- learning. *Academy of Management Learning & Education, 4*(3), 309–323.

Greiner, L. E., & Metzger, R. O. (1983). *Consulting to management*. Englewood Cliffs, NJ: Prentice-Hall.

GroupMap. SOAR analysis. Retrieved January 10, 2020 from https://www.groupmap.com/map-templates/soar-analysis/.

Gulati, R., Mayo, A. J., & Nohria, N. (2017). *Management: An integrated approach* (2nd ed.). Boston, MA: Cengage Learning.

iSixSigma. Determine the root cause: 5 whys. Retrieved January 10, 2020 from https://www.isixsigma.com/tools-templates/cause-effect/determine-root-cause-5-whys/.

Kickul, J., Griffiths, M., & Bacq, S. (2010). The boundary-less classroom: Extending social innovation and impact learning to the field. *Journal of Small Business and Enterprise Development, 17*(4), 652–663.

Lyons, B. (2003). Group diseases in the science classroom: A reference guide to symptoms and treatments. Retrieved June 5, 2003 from http://www2.canisius.edu/~morriss/bio201/groups.html.

Maskulka, T. A., Stout, D. E., & Massad, V. J. (2011). Using and assessing an experiential learning project in a retail marketing course. *Journal of Instructional Pedagogies, 6*, 1–20.

Matthews, C. (1998). The Small Business Institute Program: High impact entrepreneurship education. *Journal of Small Business Strategy, 9*(2), 14–22.

MindTools. Using the TOWS matrix: Developing strategic options from an external-internal analysis. Retrieved January 10, 2020 from https://www.mindtools.com/pages/article/newSTR_89.htm.

Morrison, M. (2014). Definition of SWOT analysis. Retrieved April 18, 2016 from https://rapidbi.com/swotanalysis/#OverviewOfSWOT.

Osterwalder, A., Pigneur, Y., Bernarda, G., & Smith, A. (2014). *Value proposition design: How to create products and services customers want*. Hoboken, NJ: John Wiley & Sons.

Pestleanalysis.com. What is PESTLE analysis? An important business analysis tool. Retrieved January 10, 2020 from https://pestleanalysis.com/what-is-pestle-analysis/.

Peterson, T. O. (2004). So you're thinking of trying problem-based learning? Three critical success factors for implementation. *Journal of Management Education, 28*(5), 630–647.

Porter, M. E. (1979). How competitive forces shape strategy. *Harvard Business Review*. Retrieved January 10, 2020 from https://hbr.org/1979/03/how-competitive-forces-shape-strategy.

Porter, M. E. (1998). *Competitive strategy: Techniques for analyzing industries and competitors*. New York: Free Press.

Porth, S. J., & Saltis, M. (1998). *Management consulting: Theory and tools for small business interventions*. Houston, TX: Dame Publications.

Rockart, J. F. (1979). Chief executives define their own data needs. *Harvard Business Review*. Retrieved January 10, 2020 from https://hbr.org/1979/03/chief-executives-define-their-own-data-needs.

Rutgers, The State University of New Jersey. (2003). Rutgers business school MBA team consulting program brochure. Retrieved June 3, 2003 from. http://business.rutgers.edu.

Scarborough, N. M., & Cornwall, J. R. (2019). *Essentials of entrepreneurship and small business management* (9th ed.). New York: Pearson.

Shewan, D. (2020). How to write a ferociously unique selling proposition. Retrieved January 10, 2020 from https://www.wordstream.com/blog/ws/2014/04/07/unique-selling-proposition.

Warters, W. (2000). Conflict resolution tools and tips for students (p. 6). Retrieved June 5, 2003 from http://www.campus-adr.org/Student_Center/tips_student.html.

Index

Note: **Bold** page numbers refer to tables and *italic* page numbers refer to figures.

For Product Safety Concerns and Information please contact our EU
representative GPSR@taylorandfrancis.com
Taylor & Francis Verlag GmbH, Kaufingerstraße 24, 80331 München, Germany

www.ingramcontent.com/pod-product-compliance
Lightning Source LLC
Chambersburg PA
CBHW062310271225
37384CB00009B/713

* 9 7 8 1 0 3 2 0 0 5 1 6 4 *